THE BALKANS
AND
NORTH AFRICA
1941 – 1942

Dust and smoke rise into the
air as German paratroops
race forward to attack a
position in Crete.

BLITZKRIEG

THE BALKANS
AND
NORTH AFRICA
1941 – 1942

WILL FOWLER

Ian Allan PUBLISHING

First published 2003

ISBN 0 7110 2946 6

Published by Ian Allan Publishing
an imprint of Ian Allan Publishing Ltd, Hersham, Surrey KT12 4RG.

Printed by Ian Allan Printing Ltd, Hersham, Surrey KT12 4RG.

Code: 0302/A2

Designed by Casebourne Rose Design Associates Ltd

Illustrations by Mike Rose
Maps by Sue Casebourne

Picture Credits
All photographs are from Bugle Archives.

COVER PICTURE: A standard bearer of the 1 *Gruppe Jagdgeschwader* 27 presents the colours in front of a Bf109 (Trop) in North Africa.

Blitzkrieg: Fast armoured and mechanised warfare supported by bombers and ground attack aircraft.

CONTENTS

UNTERNEHMEN MARITA
6-27

The German invasion of Yugoslavia, triggered by the need to rescue the Italians from their disastrous attack on Greece, was a model of co-operation between tanks and aircraft. Riven by national factionalism and hopelessly outclassed, the Yugoslav armed forces were quickly defeated.

GREEK TRAGEDY
28-43

British and Greek troops fought together against German and Italian forces, but air power was the deciding factor of the campaign. With the benefit of ULTRA intelligence, the British and Commonwealth troops of W Force were able to withdraw from Greece and German-occupied Athens.

UNTERNEHMEN MERKUR
44-65

The plans for the German airborne attack on Crete were known through ULTRA to the island's commander General Freyberg. The inadequately armed and equipped troops under his command fought hard and were close to defeating the German paratroops, but were finally forced to withdraw.

AFRIKA KORPS
ASCENDANT
66-94

German troops under General Erwin Rommel arrived in North Africa to assist the Italians who were suffering badly under attacks by British and Commonwealth forces. Under Rommel the *Afrika Korps* counter attacked and eventually pushed the 8th Army back into Egypt, where General Montgomery took a stand at El Alamein.

INDEX 95–96

UNTERNEHMEN MARITA

The military revolt in Yugoslavia has changed the political position in the Balkans. Yugoslavia, even if it makes initial professions of loyalty, must be regarded as an enemy and beaten down as quickly as possible.

Adolf Hitler

Directive No 25, March 27, 1941

Hitler had been an early admirer of the Fascist Italy of Benito Mussolini. Long before Hitler achieved power in Germany in 1933, Mussolini had begun to transform Italy into a totalitarian state.

Italy went to war to seize the African kingdom of Abyssinia in October 1935 and had expanded its territorial and colonial control through the 1930s.

As France was reeling from German attacks, Italy declared war on her on June 10, 1940. The Italian attempt to advance along the Mediterranean coast was disastrous and the depleted French forces held the attacks until the French surrender at Compiègne. The Italians were then able to grab border areas of southeastern France and extended their control as far as Lyon to the north and Avignon to the south on the River Rhone as well as the island of Corsica.

On September 27, 1940 Germany and Italy, who had already signed the Axis Pact on May

22, 1939, signed the Tripartite Pact with Japan that promised mutual assistance if one of the signatories was attacked. In November Romania, Hungary and Slovakia signed and in March 1941 Bulgaria and Yugoslavia, though following a British-engineered coup Yugoslavia repudiated it almost immediately. After the defeat of Yugoslavia the Nazi puppet state of Croatia signed on June 15, 1941.

The Tripartite Pact did not include joint measures for waging the war and left member states some leeway. Even though Italian troops had invaded the tiny and primitive kingdom of Albania as far back as April 7, 1939, Mussolini caught Hitler off guard when he announced: *"Führer* we are on the march" and informed him that Italian troops in Albania had attacked Greece on October 28, 1940. A day later the two leaders met at the Brenner Pass and Hitler, though angry at the lack of consultation, offered Mussolini the assistance of German forces. The *Duce* declined since he saw the Balkans as his sphere of influence.

At the outbreak of war in September 1939 Greece, under its authoritarian leader General Ioannis Metaxas, had adopted a policy of neutrality. In the early hours of October 28 through his ambassador in Athens Mussolini presented a calculated unacceptable ultimatum to the Greeks. Metaxas rejected it with a dignified refusal. (After the war October 28 became a national holiday celebrated as *Okhi* ["No!"] day.)

At 05.30 on Monday October 28, attacking out of Albania, the six Italian divisions of the 11th and 9th Armies under General Visconti-Prasca made some headway in four thrusts through the mountains. Accompanied by

LEFT: Gaunt and frail, Mussolini greets a shaken Hitler and congratulates him on surviving the attempt on his life in July 1944. In less than a year's time both men would be dead.

BENITO AMILCARE ANDREA MUSSOLINI
(1883 – 1945)

Born at Dovia in the province of Forli on July 29, 1883 he served as a private in World War I and was wounded in training. Following the war Mussolini established the *Fascio di Combattimento* – the Union of Combat – the Latin word *"Fasces"* from which Facism is derived was chosen from the bundle of rods encircling an axe that was used in ancient Rome by Lictors as a symbol of authority. In October 22, 1922 he led the March on Rome with 50,000 Fascists and pressurised the government into making him Prime Minister. Hitler took the march as the model for his Beer Hall Putsch.

The parades, salutes and uniforms of the Italians were adopted by the Nazis. When Hitler visited Mussolini in Italy it was as an up and coming politician visiting an established national leader. Italian and German troops served in Spain in the Civil War but when Mussolini took Italy into the war on the side of Germany in 1940, this exposed the poor quality of the equipment and training of the armed forces. Italian troops suffered losses in Greece, Albania, North Africa and Russia. On July 25, 1943, following the Allied invasion of mainland Italy, Mussolini was sacked by King Victor Emmanuel. Under German control an Italian Fascist state hung on in northern Italy. At the close of the war, attempting to escape into Switzerland with his mistress Clara Petacci, Mussolini was captured by Italian partisans and executed on April 28, 1945. Their bodies were hung up in a public square in Milan.

Albanian troops and volunteers they were ostensibly on a mission of "liberation" for Albanians living in Greece.

They faced four Greek divisions of the 1st Army. Though on paper the Greeks appeared outnumbered their divisions were larger, at 18,500 in contrast to the Italians, at between 12,000 and 14,000. The Greeks had more efficient light and medium artillery and more machine guns. They stopped the Italian attacks and then on November 4 the 2nd

ABOVE: The Italian crew of a Mitriaglice Fiat 194/35 machine gun man the weapon in an anti-aircraft role. The gun, dating from World War I, was unreliable and unpopular.

Corps under Colonel Papadopoulos counter attacked the Italian 11th Army under General Gelsos. The Greek Army of Macedonia inflicted a startling defeat on the elite Italian *Iulia* Mountain Division

Greek forces recaptured border areas and

GREECE

| **C-in-C General** | 4 Fighter Sqns |
| Papagos | 3 Bomber Sqns |

ARMY	**NAVY**
500,000 men	2,900 men
18 Infantry	1 Cruiser
Divisions	10 Destroyers
	13 Torpedo
AIR FORCE	Boats
3,000 men	6 Submarines
120 aircraft	

LEFT: An Italian flame thrower crew in action. Both weapons, clothing and equipment were unsuitable for the type of fighting and harsh terrain over which Italian forces would be operating in Greece.

forced the Italians out of Greece and across the border into Albania. By mid-November they had deployed 11 infantry divisions, two infantry brigades and one cavalry division against 15 Italian infantry divisions and one tank division.

Mussolini's generals had warned him against launching an attack in this harsh terrain so late in the year. His Chief of Staff Marshal Pietro Badoglio resigned in protest and on December 4 his Under Secretary of State for War, General Ubaldo Soddu, recommended an armistice with the Greeks.

On February 23, 1941 the Greek government under Alexandros Korizis accepted the offer of British military assistance. Known as W Force after its commander Lt General Maitland Wilson it consisted of 50,672 men from the New Zealand Division, and 6th and 7th Australian Divisions of the 1st Australian Corps under Lt General Blamey. In addition armour and artillery support was also drawn from the Middle East Command of General Wavell in Egypt. This was a sizeable slice of Wavell's force that was fighting hard against the Italians in North Africa. In Operation *Lustre* W Force sailed for Greece and on March 4 began landing at Piraeus.

By March 1 the Greek forces had captured Porto Edda on the coast and the inland towns of Klisura, Koritsa, Pogradec and were within striking distance of the Albanian capital Tirana.

The submarines in the small Greek Navy lay in wait in the waters of the Adriatic and sank 18 Italian ships carrying men, stores and equipment from Italy to Albania.

The Italian navy was also suffering humiliating losses in action against the Royal Navy in the Mediterranean. In Operation *Judgement* on November 11, 1940, for the loss of two aircraft, 12 Fleet Air Arm Swordfish torpedo bombers operating from the carrier HMS *Illustrious* 290km (180 miles) off the

SAVOIA-MARCHETTI SM79-II SPARVIERO (SPARROWHAWK)

The three-engined aircraft was originally designed as an airliner and saw action in the Spanish Civil War. It was used as both a conventional and torpedo bomber. It was a rugged machine that handled well and between 1939 and 1944 some 1,200 aircraft of all types were built. Over 100 were exported and a Rumanian built version powered by two 1,220hp Junkers engines saw action on the Eastern Front.

Type:	Bomber
Crew:	4 – 5
Power Plant:	Three 780hp Alfa Romeo 126 RC 34
Performance:	Maximum speed at 4,000m (13,120ft) 430km/h (267mph)
Normal range:	1,900km (1,180 miles)
Weights:	Loaded 10,480kg (23,100lb)
Dimensions:	Wing span: 21.2m (69ft 6in)
	Length: 15.8m (51ft 10in)
	Height: 4.31m (14ft 1in)
Armament:	One fixed forward-firing 12.7mm (0.5in) Breda SAFAT MG; one flexible 12.7mm (0.5in) Breda SAFAT MG in dorsal and ventral position; one 7.7mm Lewis MG in either of two lateral hatches; max bomb load 1,250kg (2,750lb)

ABOVE: An Italian Air Force SM81 *Pipistrello* (Bat), a military version of the SM73 airliner that was used as a utility aircraft.

RIGHT: The Italian battleship *Conte de Cavour* badly damaged at Taranto.

Italian coast had crippled three battleships and a cruiser and damaged dock installations in the Italians' base at Taranto. The attack at night was undertaken in two waves. Each wave had two aircraft that dropped flares to illuminate the targets. Following the attack the Italian fleet moved north to harbours on Italy's west coast, reducing their ability to attack British convoys in the Mediterranean.

The operation was later closely studied by the Imperial Japanese Navy who were interested to establish if aerial torpedoes would run true in the confined waters of a harbour. It was clear that they would, and so similar tactics would be used at Pearl Harbor in their attack against the American Pacific Fleet on Sunday December 7, 1941.

On February 25, 1941 the submarine HMS *Upholder* sank the cruiser *Armando Diaz* off Tunisia.

The naval action was not completely one sided however. On March 26 Italian *Mezzi Navali d'Assalto* one-man high-speed craft loaded with explosives were used in a spectacular attack against the cruiser HMS *York* in Suda Bay, Crete. The warship was crippled and later sunk by German bombers.

Italian *Maiale* – "Pig" – submersibles crippled the battleships HMS *Queen Elizabeth* and *Valiant* in Alexandria harbour on December 19, 1941. The Pigs were 6.7m (22ft) long and had a two-man crew equipped with dry suits and breathing equipment, who sat astride them like a giant tandem motorcycle. The Human Torpedo, as the British dubbed them, had a detachable warhead that could be positioned underneath the keel of an anchored ship. A timer on the warhead allowed the crew to swim clear and escape. In Alexandria the Italian "frog men", as the swimmers in their black waterproof one-piece suits were nicknamed, were captured but remained

ABOVE: The thick armour of British Matilda Mk II tanks was a frightening shock for Italian gunners in North Africa who were forced to aim for the tracks.

silent until the charges had exploded beneath the two battleships.

ULTRA intelligence allowed the British Mediterranean Fleet to intercept an Italian task force of eight cruisers, nine destroyers and the battleship *Vittorio Veneto*. Aircraft

SELLING AGGRESSION

At 5.30 this morning the German Government announced that it felt compelled to order the *Wehrmacht* to march into Greece and Yugoslavia last night, with the aim of driving Britain out of Europe once and for all.

German News Bureau
Sunday April 6, 1941, Berlin

from HMS *Formidable* damaged *Vittorio Veneto* and the British warships under Admiral Cunningham sank two heavy cruisers and two destroyers, while the damaged Italian heavy cruiser *Pola* was later torpedoed. The action on March 28, 1941, known as the battle of Cape Matapan, marked the high point of Royal Navy operations in the Mediterranean.

Earlier in North Africa on September 13, 1940 80,000 men of the Italian 10th Army grouped in five divisions supported by 200 tanks pushed over the border from the Italian colony of Tripolitania into British-protected Egypt.

It was counter attacked in December 10 – 11 by a fast-moving and vigorously led British and Commonwealth force of 30,000 commanded by General Archibald Wavell and forced back into Libya. On February 7 at Beda Fomm a pincer movement caught the withdrawing Italians and by the end of their campaign they had lost 130,000 troops, 845 guns and 380 tanks while British and Commonwealth losses were 2,000 men.

ABOVE: South African gunners training with obsolescent 18-Pounder guns that would be replaced by the superb 25-Pounder Gun Howitzer.

LEFT: Defences dug into the side of a wadi for cover and camouflage.

FRENCH HUMOUR

In Vichy and Occupied France, among the jokes that circulated, was a fictional telephone call from Hitler to Mussolini following the failure of the Italian attack on Greece.

"Benito aren't you in Athens yet?"

"I can't hear you Adolf."

"I said aren't you in Athens yet?"

"I can't hear you. You must be ringing from a long way off, presumably London."

Germany's flamboyant Italian ally was becoming a liability.

Hitler was well advanced in his plans for the invasion of Russia so when in March 1941 British troops and aircraft arrived in Greece he feared that his right flank would be insecure. Rumania was now supplying Germany with the bulk of its fuel and oil requirements from the Ploesti oil fields and bombers based in a hostile Greece could easily reach Rumania. In 1939 Germany had imported 848,000 tons of oil from Rumania, this had risen to 1,177,000 tons in 1940 and in the year that she invaded the USSR (1941) it stood at a wartime record of 2,963,000 tons. The USSR had provided Germany with 617,000 tons in 1940 and so helped fuel the tanks that crashed through Western Europe.

The fastest and most effective way to prevent the threat of air attacks on Ploesti was to neutralise Greece. The original operation in a directive issued by Hitler in December 13, 1940 called for the occupation of the Aegean coast and Salonika Basin. In the end the Germans with their Italian allies would

seize not only mainland Greece, but also the offshore islands.

A passive or cooperative Yugoslavia was necessary for German troops to move south. The Yugoslav government in Belgrade was strong-armed by the Germans and Italians into joining the Tripartite Pact on March 25. However, two days later, encouraged by the British Foreign Office, Serbian officers in the Air Force led a coup against the government of Prince Paul, rejecting the Pact and setting up a government of national unity under

FAR LEFT, ABOVE AND BELOW: Heinkel He111 bombers part of the force that devastated Belgrade in three waves of attacks on Easter Sunday, 1941.

LEFT: The crew of a PzKpfw II watch nervously as the driver manoeuvres across a flooded river in Yugoslavia during the German invasion.

BELOW: Heavily laden *Gebirgsjäger* mountain troops advance into Yugoslavia. The Royal Yugoslav Army was completely outclassed in equipment and training by the German invaders.

General Dusan Simovic with the 17-year-old Prince Peter as monarch. Hitler was enraged. To him the Pact was perfectly reasonable. Yugoslavia would offer German troops free passage to attack Greece and for this she would have been able to seize the Greek province of Salonika.

He ordered an air attack, aptly named Operation *Punishment*, against the completely unprotected capital, Belgrade. Flying in three waves 484 bombers and dive bombers with 250 fighter escorts hit the Yugoslav capital on April 6, Easter Sunday, in a succession of 20-minute attacks. The figures killed vary considerably from 5,000 to 17,000 in what was a supposedly open city.

ABOVE: A Junkers Ju88 runs up its engines on an improvised airstrip. The Ju88 was one of the outstanding aircraft of World War II, operating in a variety of roles including fighter, bomber and dive bomber.

ORDERS – COUNTER ORDERS – DISORDER

"All troops must engage the enemy wherever encountered and with every means at their disposal. Do not wait for direct orders from above but act on your own and be guided by your judgement, initiative and conscience."

Yugoslav General Dusan Simovic
Radio orders to the Army April 1941

What is certain is the attacks panicked the young king and his government into flight. During the raids the fighter squadrons of the Royal Yugoslav Air Force took off to defend the city. Some were equipped with Hawker Hurricanes, others had Messerschmitt Bf109s. They shot down two aircraft but by the end of the campaign out of 419 aircraft the air force had lost 49 in the air and 85 on the ground with about 50 escaping to Greece and some later making their way to Egypt. At 05.10 on April 6 *Luftflotte* IV under General Löhr attacked airfields in Yugoslavia as well as Belgrade.

The Yugoslav plan of operations "R-41", like that adopted by Poland in 1939, played into the German hands. It called for defence of the entire length of the border in which almost the whole army, 27 divisions, would be tied up. The only offensive operation envisaged was with Greek forces on the Albanian border against the Italians.

On land the German 2nd Army under General Freiherr von Weichs attacked from Austria on April 6 and at 05.30 on April 8 General von Kleist's *Panzergruppe* I, that had been earmarked for an attack on Thrace in Greece, pushed towards Belgrade from Bulgaria. In brief fighting the *Panzergruppe* smashed the right wing of the Yugoslav 5th Army. A day later it took the town Nis and turned to attack Belgrade driving through the Yugoslav 6th Army that was holding the Morava river valley. The XIV *Panzer Korps* reached Skopje on April 8, and German troops entered Nis.

The German 12th Army attacked Thrace, detaching the XL *Panzer Korps* westward through the Vardar region of southern Yugoslavia that led to Macedonia and the Monastir gap. On April 10 it linked up with Italian forces on Lake Ochrid and moved into positions where it could attack Greece from the north.

Luftwaffe bombers based in Bulgaria attacked the Greek port of Piraeus and hit the SS *Clan Fraser*, a freighter loaded with ammunition for the British Expeditionary Force. The huge explosion that followed wrecked the port.

On April 12 German and Italian forces moved towards Greece. The Italian V, VI and XI Corps was backed by *Luftflotte* IV that attacked the Yugoslav 7th Army columns and troop concentrations around the Ljubljana area. The Italians encountered little resistance from the enemy who were attempting to withdraw to the southeast. Around 30,000 Yugoslav troops concentrated near Delnice to await the Italians to make their surrender.

On April 13, in a daring coup, Belgrade was captured by motorcycle reconnaissance

BELOW: The commander of an SdKfz 231 armoured car watches as it fords a stream in Yugoslavia. The bullet-proof tyres could be removed to allow it to drive along railway tracks.

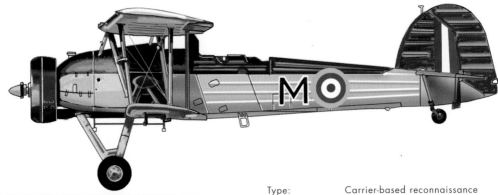

FAIREY SWORDFISH MK I

The Swordfish entered service with the Fleet Air Arm in 1936. It remained in action throughout the war, actually outlasting the aircraft that was designed to replace it. The biplane construction of the Swordfish earned it the affectionate nickname "Stringbag" and its outdated canvas construction proved very resilient with contact-fused cannon shells actually passing through without exploding. Fairey built 2,400 Swordfish in World War II.

Type:	Carrier-based reconnaissance /torpedo-bomber
Crew:	2 - 3
Power Plant:	One 690hp Bristol Pegasus IIIM3
Performance:	Maximum speed 248km/h (154mph)
Maximum range:	1,657km (1,030 miles)
Weights:	Empty 1,903kg (4,195lb)
	Loaded 3,502kg (7,720lb)
Dimensions:	Wing span 13.87m (45ft 6in)
	Length 10.87m (35ft 8in)
	Height 3.76m (12ft 4in)
Armament:	One fixed .303in Vickers MG firing through the propeller hub; one .303in Lewis or Vickers K gun; provision for one 18in torpedo or 680kg (1,500lb) mine or one 680kg (1,500lb) bomb.

troops of the *Waffen-SS* Division *Reich*, part of the XLI *Panzer Korps*. The commander of this assault group, *SS-Hauptsturmführer* Klingenberg, had found all the bridges across the Danube had been demolished but captured a motor boat and after a hazardous journey entered the city and took the surrender from the mayor. Klingenberg also hoisted the swastika over the German legation and released a representative of the German Foreign Ministry who had been interned by the Yugoslavs. For this coup he was awarded the Knight's Cross. Klingenberg would rise to command a division and die in fighting in the West in 1945.

There was some confusion over who had captured Belgrade since three separate attacks were converging on the Yugoslav capital. The 8th Panzer Division, part of the German 2nd Army, was off the air for nearly

GIOVINEZZA EROICA

ABOVE: A grimly heroic postcard produced in Italy shows a machine gunner dying at his post.

RIGHT: Yugoslavia did not stand a chance when German forces attacked from two sides. The Italian navy controlled the seas to the west and the *Luftwaffe* dominated the skies. Yugoslav tactics played into German hands as they attempted to hold the frontiers and so were cut off or bypassed.

MILES

0   25   50   75

0   50   100 150 200 250
KILOMETRES

GER 2 ARMY

Danube   • Budapest

Graz

XLIX MTN
CORPS   LI CORPS   **HUNGARY**

XLVI PZ CORPS   • Szeged

HUN 3 ARMY

• Trieste   ZAGREB   Drava   • Timisoara   XLI MTR
CORPS   **ROMANIA**

Fiume •

Sava   • Novisad

Zemun •   • BELGRADE

YUGOSLAVIA

Zara •   • Kragujevac   Danube

Sibenik •   Sarajevo •   • Uzice
Split •   • Krusevac   XI CORPS

ADRIATIC SEA   Drina   XIV PZ CORPS

Dubrovnik •   4 ITAL
DIVS   • SOFIA
XL PZ
CORPS   **BULGARIA**

ALBANIA   Skopje •   XVIII
CORPS   XXX
CORPS

ITALY   Tirane •   • Strumica

Monastir •   • Salonika

• Naples   ITAL 9, 11
ARMIES   • Kozani

• Taranto   GR 1 ARMY   Trikkala   • Larisa   **AEGEAN SEA**
Ioannina •

GREECE

Lamia •

IONIAN SEA   Mesolongion •   Thebes •   • Rafina

Patrai •   ATHENS •   • Porto Rafti
Corinth •

SICILY   • Nauplia

Kalamata •   • Monemvasia

British evacuation routes

MALTA   **CRETE**

Legend:
→ German attacks
→ Italian attacks
→ Hungarian attacks
— Metaxas line
▲▲▲ Aliakmon line
•••• Front line at date shown
⊙ German air-borne landing May 26
✈ Luftwaffe forward air fields

ABOVE: A PzKpfwIII fords a river, bypassing a demolished bridge on the Yugoslav border.

LEFT: German soldiers take cover behind concrete anti-tank obstacles on the Greek Bulgarian border.

24 hours and then at 11.52 on April 13 the division's operations officer reported: "During the night the 8.Panzer-Division drove into Belgrade, occupied the city, and hoisted the Swastika flag".

However, the 2nd Army had better communications with *Panzergruppe* 1, who signalled before the 8th Panzer Division: "*Panzergruppe von Kleist*' has taken Belgrade from the south. Patrols of *Infanterie*-Regiment

'*Gross Deutschland*' have entered the city from the north. With General von Kleist at the head, the 11 Panzer-Division has been rolling into the capital since 06.32".

The final drive of the campaign was on the historic city of Sarajevo. The commander of the German 2nd Army, General von Weichs, was aware that the mountainous terrain in the area would be ideal for waging a prolonged campaign. Bad weather and poor

RIGHT: German mountain troops lead mules laden with radio equipment along a mountain track in Greece. The *Gebirgsjäger* were experienced climbers recruited from southern Germany and Austria.

CROAT VOLUNTEERS

Croatia – a country that had seen itself as the victim of Serb oppression – was delighted when it was recognised as an independent country. It contributed ground forces to assist the Germans as well as a small naval force operating in the Aegean and air force squadrons that fought on the eastern Front. These squadrons produced a number of aces.

Verstärktes Infanterie Regiment 369 (kroatisches)

The *Verstärktes Infanterie* Regiment 369 (*kroatisches*) also known as the Croatian Legion (*Hrvatska Legija*) was formed soon after the German invasion of the Soviet Union. It was made up of two companies of Croatian and one company of Bosnian volunteers and was posted to Döllersheim, Austria, for training.

It was attached to the 100 *Jäger* Division and was sent to Army Group South on the Eastern front. The regiment fought at Valki, Kharkov, Kalatch and at the Don before being trapped and destroyed in Stalingrad.

1. Light Infantry Parachute Battalion

1. Light Infantry Parachute Battalion (1. *Padobranska Lovacka Bonja*) was formed in 1942 as 1. Light Infantry Parachute Company (1. *Padobranska Lovacka Sat*). The volunteers were trained at the Air Force school at Petrovaradin before moving to the new training area at Koprivnica. The base was attacked by the partisans in October 1943 and the paratroopers were forced out after days of heavy fighting, where they suffered 20 killed or captured.

Following the attack the unit was disbanded. It was, however, soon reformed again and expanded to battalion size. It was sent to the area of Resnik and Obrovo in January 1945 to fight the partisans. The unit later fought the partisans at Sisak and Petrinja, this time attached to the *Kampfgruppe Schlacher* (*Borbena Skupina Schlacher*) together with the Motorised *Brigade (Brzi Zdrug)*.

At the end of the war the men of this unit marched to Austria and surrendered to the Allies but were immediately transferred back to the partisans and most of them were killed.

MACCHI MC200 SAETTA (DART)

First flown in 1937, the MC200 was developed from the racing seaplanes that had been designed to compete for speed trophies in the 1930s. A rugged design, its weakness was the radial engine. Only when a German liquid-cooled engine was fitted to the C202 *Folgore* (Thunderbolt) and a 1,475hp engine to the C205 *Veltro* (Greyhound) did the *Regia Aeronautica* have fighters that could take on types like the USAAF P51D. Only 262 C205s were built and these were taken over by the *Luftwaffe* after September 1943.

Type:	Fighter
Crew:	1
Power Plant:	One 870hp Fiat A.74 RC38
Performance:	Maximum speed at 4,500m (14,765ft) 502km/h (312mph)
Maximum range:	870km (540 miles)
Weights:	Empty 1,800kg (3,902lb) Loaded 2,200kg (4,850lb)
Dimensions:	Wing span 10.58m (34ft 8in) Length 8.19m (26ft 10in) Height 3.51m (11ft 6in)
Armament:	Two 12.7mm (0.5in) Breda SAFAT MGs in upper cowling

roads had delayed the Germans but if the Yugoslavs offered more resistance in these mountains, fighting could last for months. The 2nd Army was reorganised into two pursuit groups to keep up the pressure on the Yugoslavs.

Under the command of the recently arrived LII Infantry Corps HQ, the western group consisted of four infantry divisions under the XLIX Corps and LI Corps as well as the 14th Panzer Division.

The eastern force under *Panzergruppe* I was made up of six divisions with the 8th Panzer Division leading the drive towards Sarajevo from the east. *Luftflotte* IV was tasked with neutralising the anticipated enemy troop concentrations in the Mostar-Sarajevo sector.

By the evening of April 13, as the 14th Panzer Division approached Sarajevo, reports reached the Germans of fighting between Serbs and Croats in Mostar. German aircraft

were diverted to attack the Serb positions. A day later fighting between these groups had spread to the whole of Dalmatia.

On April 15 both pursuit groups of the 2nd Army were closing in on Sarajevo. As two Panzer divisions entered simultaneously from east and west the Yugoslav 2nd Army, which had its HQ in the city, capitulated.

Four days after the fall of Belgrade an unconditional surrender was signed by the Yugoslavs at 21.00 on Thursday April 17. General von Weichs signed for the Germans, the Italian military attaché in Belgrade for the Italians and a Hungarian liaison officer was present but did not sign since technically his country was "not at war with Yugoslavia". The Yugoslav government was represented by Foreign Minister Cincar-Marcovic and the armed forces by General Milojko Yankovic.

It was a move that marked the dismantling of Yugoslavia and creation of the puppet state of Croatia. Areas of Slovenia were annexed

FIAT G50BIS *FRECCIA* (ARROW)

An attractive and well designed aircraft, the two major faults of the G50 were a light armament and underpowered engine. It saw action in Spain and in the Balkans and North Africa. The soundness of the aircraft's design was proved with the cannon-armed G55 *Centauro* (Centaur) that married the airframe to a 1,475hp liquid-cooled engine. The G55 entered production in 1943 and only 105 were built.

Type:	Fighter/fighter-bomber
Crew:	1
Power Plant:	One 840hp Fiat A.74 RC 38
Performance:	Maximum speed at 4,500m (14,765ft) 470km/h (293mph)
	Normal range 676km (420 miles)
Weights:	Empty 2,015kg (4,443lb)
	Loaded 2,522kg (5,560lb)
Dimensions:	Wing span 10.9m (36ft)
	Length 7.8m (25ft 7in)
	Height 2.95m (9ft 8in)
Armament:	Two fixed forward-firing 12.7mm (0.5in) Breda SAFAT MGs in fuselage; max bomb load 300kg (660lb)

ABOVE: Ground crew warm the engines of a Fiat BR.20M *Cicogna* (Stork) bomber prior to takeoff. The BR.20 saw action in the Battle of Britain as well as the Mediterranean and Eastern Front.

by Italy or incorporated into the Greater German *Reich*. On the Dalmatian coast the Italians took Zara as a naval base and many of the offshore islands as well as Kotor to the south. They administered the state of Montenegro, their puppet Albania and grabbed areas of Kosovo and western Macedonia. The Bulgarians seized Skopje,

Veles and Macedonia. To the north and east the Germans administered Serbia and occupied Banat with its German-speaking minority, while Hungary took the provinces of Backa, Prekmurje and Medjumurje.

In Directive No 26 issued on April 4, 1941 Hitler had already cynically anticipated these land grabs and that Yugoslavia's Balkan

ABOVE: Waving white flags Yugoslav soldiers hesitantly cross a stream to surrender to German forces. The ethnic mix of the Yugoslav army split it into factions, some of which were actually pro-German.

ABOVE: Pro-Axis crowds in Croatia greet the crew of a German BMW R75 motorcycle combination from a reconnaissance unit.

neighbours could out of self interest thus be called on to act in concert with German forces or at least grant them free passage.

The Fascist organisation *Ustasa* led by Ante Pavelic ran the Independent State of Croatia or *Drzava Hrvatska Nezavisna* (DHN) that had been set up by the Germans. They waged a particularly brutal war against the Serbs within Croatia, expelling, murdering or converting them to Roman Catholicism in roughly equal numbers. Incredibly Croatia was actually a kingdom with a monarch – the Italian Duke of Spoleto – who during the brief life of his kingdom never visited his lands or his subjects. During the fighting in Yugoslavia some Croat units had refused to go into action against the Germans. One German formation surprised a Croat unit that was still in garrison and not yet fully mobilised. A regimental officers' party which was in progress was interrupted only long enough to sign the instruments of surrender, then the officers returned to drinking as if nothing untoward had happened.

With the invasion of the USSR four months

THE OPPOSING FORCES

Bulgaria

Army
650,000 men
13 Infantry Divisions
2 Mobile Divisions

Air Force
100 aircraft
18 Sqns

Navy
4 Patrol Boats

Yugoslavia

Army
1,400,000 men
110 light tanks

Air Force
419 aircraft
1 Fighter Wing
1 Bomber Wing
7 Sqns Army
Aviation (obsolete)

Navy
1 Cruiser (old)
4 Destroyers
16 Torpedo Boats
4 Submarines

Hungary

Army
700,000 men
12 Infantry Divisions
2 Armoured Divisions
1 Light Division
1 Cavalry Division

Air Force
1,000 aircraft
8 Fighter Sqns
8 Bomber Sqns
13 Reconnaissance
Sqns

Navy
6 Picket ships
7 Auxiliary boats

ABOVE: Yugoslav prisoners of war wait to hear their fate. Many were released following the defeat.

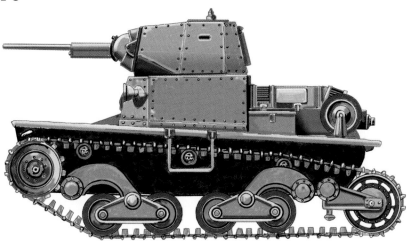

FIAT L6/40 LIGHT TANK

The little Fiat tank was roughly the equivalent of the German PzKpfw II when it was introduced in 1939. Though 283 were built and it saw service in cavalry and reconnaissance units in Italy, North Africa and Russia, it was never an ideal front line vehicle. The hull was modified as a flame thrower, a command tank with extra radios and an open topped turret, and a less than successful assault gun.

Armament:	One Breda Model 35 20mm (0.78in) cannon; one coaxial Breda Model 38 8mm (0.31in) MG
Armour:	6-40mm (0.23in-1.57in)
Crew:	2
Weight:	6,800kg (6.69 ton)
Hull length:	3.78m (12ft 5in)
Width:	1.92m (6ft 4in)
Height:	2.03m (6ft 8in)
Engine:	One SPA 18D four-cylinder petrol engine developing 70hp
Road speed:	42km/h (26mph)
Range:	200km (124 miles)

later, Croatia initially committed a reinforced infantry regiment to join the German forces.

With Bulgaria within the Nazi orbit the Greek defences – the Metaxas Line – could now be outflanked. Under King Boris III Bulgaria joined in the attack on Yugoslavia and grabbed territory on its borders, but when Germany invaded the USSR they did not participate. Bulgarian soldiers did however join the anti-partisan drives against Tito's forces in Yugoslavia.

One of the little reported actions of the Yugoslav campaign was the so called "*Feuezauber*" operations on the Austrian-

LEFT: A 3.7cm Pak 35/36 crew covers the border between Bulgaria and Greece. The gun was inadequate against British Matilda II tanks and would be hopeless against Soviet T-34s.

FIAT M13/40 MEDIUM TANK

The first examples of the Carro Armato M13/40 appeared in North Africa in December 1941. Its 47mm gun had good penetrative power and outranged the British 2pdr. Both the British and Australian forces used captured tanks, the latter painting bold kangaroo motifs on the hull. At one stage 100 were in Allied service. The chassis was later used as the basis for the Semovente M40 da 75 assault gun and the Carro Commando command tank.

Armament:	One 47mm (1.85in) gun; two Modello 38 8mm (0.31in) MGs
Armour:	6-42mm (0.24-1.65in)
Crew:	4
Weight:	14,000kg (13.78 tons)
Hull length:	4.92m (16ft 2in)
Width:	2.2m (7ft 3in)
Height:	2.38m (7ft 10in)
Engine:	One SPA TM40 eight-cylinder diesel engine developing 125hp
Road speed:	32km/h (20mph)
Range:	200km (125miles)

Yugoslav border. The terrain did not lend itself to operations by motorised units but a force of HQ staff and recently conscripted soldiers were assembled on the border. It consisted of four battalion staffs, nine rifle companies, two *Gebirgsjäger* pioneer platoons with two *Gebirgsjäger* artillery batteries, one SP medium artillery battery, four anti-tank companies, three signal and four bicycle platoons. The task was to secure the start line for the 2nd Army under General von Weichs. They adopted a much more aggressive approach to their mission. For the loss of one killed and two wounded, one group under Hauptmann Palten made an assault river crossing and entered Maribor, capturing over 100 prisoners and weapons and equipment. Palten was then ordered to take his force back to the border and resume his more static duties.

ABOVE: An Italian propaganda postcard celebrates heroic death in Africa.

GREEK TRAGEDY

Following violent attack and pursuit fighting, German Panzer
Division spearheads pursued the fleeing British and marched into
Athens at 09.25 on Sunday.
The Swastika flag has been hoisted over the Acropolis

Oberkommando der Wehrmacht
Sunday April 27, 1941

The German attack on Greece that began on April 8 was to be quick and ruthless. The 12th Army under General Wilhem von List pierced the Greek defences in Thrace and on April 9 the 2nd Panzer Division under General Veiel took

Salonika. However, poor roads, bad weather and crucially hard fighting by the Greek armies and British Expeditionary Force imposed delays on the Germans.

The Greek 2nd Army holding the Metaxas Line that ran from the Aegean to the border

with Yugoslavia and protected northern Greece and Salonika was outflanked by attacks through Yugoslavia. Trapped and bombarded it was finally forced to surrender.

Frontal attacks on the line by the XVIII *Gebirgsjäger* Corps had met with extremely tough resistance even after three days of attacks supported by artillery and dive bombers. The intensity of the fighting can be gauged by the fact that in the Rupul Gorge the German 125th Infantry Regiment suffered such heavy casualties that it was rendered combat ineffective.

The Greek 2nd Army surrendered on April 9 and after the soldiers had been disarmed the Germans released them.

By the morning of April 10 the 40th Panzer Corps had pushed through the Monastir Gap from Yugoslavia. The first contact with W Force happened on April 11 when a *Waffen-SS* reconnaissance unit entered Vevi but was halted by Australian troops holding ground covering the pass to the south. It took a day to build up a picture of the enemy position and then at dusk the *Waffen-SS* attacked and broke through the defile.

During the early afternoon of April 13 the 9th Panzer Division's 33rd Panzer Regiment entered Ptolemais, a town half way between

LEFT: With Mt Olympus in the background the crew of an MG34 on an AA mount scans the skies for RAF aircraft. One man holds the mount to keep it stable.

ABOVE: A PzKpfw III is unloaded from a freighter. Within Europe Germany was able to use the road and rail network to move men and equipment to fronts and embarkation ports.

RIGHT: A PzKpfw IV moves carefully along a mountain track in the Balkans. Poor roads and demolitions as well as fierce Greek and British resistance caused many delays.

SdKfz 222

The compact SdKfz 222 light reconnaissance vehicle entered service with the German army in 1939. At the close of the war when 1,801 had been built there were still 601 serving in the front line. The engines were uprated twice during this period. Variants included the radio vehicle the SdKfz 223 and a mobile command post the SdKfz 247 that was unarmed except for the crew's personal weapons.

Armament:	One 2cm (0.79in) or 2.8cm (1.1in) cannon; one 7.92mm (0.31in) MG
Armour:	14.5mm (0.57in) max
Crew:	3
Dimensions:	Length 4.8m (15ft 9in); Width 1.95m (6ft 4in); Height 1.8m (5ft 11in)
Weight:	4,800kg (4.72 tons)
Powerplant:	Horch V-8 petrol, 81bhp or 90bhp
Speed:	75km/h (46.6mph) road
Range:	280km (174 miles) road

Vevi and Kozani. It was here that W Force had prepared positions and the Germans came under heavy artillery fire from positions in the hills and to the southeast of Ptolemais. The reconnaissance patrols pushed forward and found the main bridge had been blown and that a water-filled ditch 1.8m (6ft) wide and 0.9m (3ft) deep with soft banks that ran across low ground was an effective anti-tank obstacle.

Under fire from the British the reconnaissance troops from 33rd Panzer Regiment identified two possible axes for advance along minor roads. Closer examination revealed that one was impassable because a bridge had been blown. The other route through marshy ground across drainage ditches was under enemy observation.

GO TELL THE SPARTANS

In 480BC 5,000 Greeks held the pass at Thermopylae against 100,000 Persians under Xerxes. The Greeks held for three days then a traitor showed the Persians a flanking route through another pass. Leonidas I of Sparta with 300 men fought a valiant rearguard action that allowed other Greeks to escape, but all 300 Spartans were killed. Xerxes was finally defeated at the great naval battle of Salamis, where the Greek forces under commander Themistocles sank 300 ships for the loss of 40.

ABOVE: Ground crew ready a Heinkel He111. Efficiently and aggressively directed air power would be decisive in the Balkans campaign both against land targets and shipping.

LEFT: Leading mules, German mountain troops move into Greece, their ski caps, cleated boots and *edelweiss* insignia were distinctive.

Choosing the route through the marsh the German tanks were forced to advance at walking speed and lost seven vehicles that got bogged down. At dusk the surviving German tanks were through and launched an attack at less than 183m (200yd) from the flank on British armour and anti-tank gun positions. Some British tanks were knocked out or abandoned and supply vehicles captured, but the delaying action had been effective. The Germans halted, low on fuel and ammunition, and waited for the bogged-down tanks to be recovered. The 33rd Panzer Regiment lost two PzKpfw IVs, one PzKpfw II and one PzKpfw I in what was the only tank action of the campaign.

On the morning of April 14 the spearheads of the 9th Panzer Division reached Kozani and established a bridgehead across the Aliakmon River. However, they had reached

ABOVE: Captured Greek vehicles on the waterfront at Kavalla in the northern Aegean. The Germans were greatly assisted in their advance by capturing abandoned British stores of fuel and rations.

the Aliakmon Line defended by W Force and for three days the Panzer division was stalled in front on these well-sited positions.

To the west the Greek 1st Army that had fought heroically in Albania was now at risk of being cut off by the rapid advance of German armour via Florina and the British withdrawal to the Aliakmon Line. From April 13 the Greeks began to pull back towards the Pindus Mountains. At Kastoria Pass they encountered the advanced guard of the German 73rd Infantry Division and fought hard for a day to break through.

On April 19 the *Waffen-SS* Regiment 1 that

ABOVE: Greek infantry with youthful admirers. The performance of the Greek Army in Albania and Greece in the winter of 1941was outstanding, earning admiration from key neutrals like the USA.

LEFT: A road becomes a stream in the spring rains in Greece. The German motorcycle crews are protected against the rain and spray by their excellent double-breasted, full-length rubberised coats.

had reached Grevena was ordered to move on a south-east axis towards Yannina to cut off the Greek 1st Army grouped as the Army of Epirus and Army of Macedonia. A day later at the Metsovon Pass high in the Pindus Mountains Greek and German forces clashed in a desperate battle. Realising that further fighting would only cause unnecessary losses

TOP LEFT: Big Short Sunderland flying boats assisting in the evacuation of key British personnel from Greece. ULTRA intercepts gave Allied planners the chance to second guess the Germans and evacuate troops from safe locations.

LEFT: German soldiers lend a hand to a motorcycle crew as they manoeuvre their BMW R75 across rugged terrain in Greece. It had a drive through to the sidecar wheel, a crew of three and an MG34 machine gun.

ABOVE: British soldiers pause by the roadside during the evacuation of Greece. The trees and other vegetation provide camouflage from the ever present *Luftwaffe* reconnaissance aircraft and bombers.

the Greek commander surrendered his forces. On Hitler's orders this was kept secret from the Italians and in recognition of their valour the officers were permitted to keep their side arms. The soldiers were disarmed and permitted to return home.

Mussolini, however, insisted that the 1st Army should also surrender to the Italians, with whom the Greeks had fought for a further two days. On April 23 the Greek commander signed a second surrender agreement that included the Italians.

On April 19 the Greeks agreed that W Force should be evacuated. On the same day men of the German XVIII *Gebirgsjäger* Corps entered Larissa and captured the airfield and British supply dumps. Ten truck loads of rations and fuel allowed the mountain troops to keep up their advance. At the port of Volos,

RIGHT: Junkers Ju52 transports that could carry 18 paratroops were used at Corinth and in large numbers in Crete.

LEFT: The German parachute design had no risers and so the soldier could not steer it and made an uncomfortable "forward roll" landing.

ABOVE: The dramatic diving "crucifix" or in modern terms "spread stable" exit from a Ju52 was essential to ensure that the paratrooper was clear of the tailplane before his parachute deployed.

which fell on April 21, the Germans again captured large quantities of petrol, oil and lubricants (POL). These captures were invaluable for the Germans whose supply lines were restricted by bad roads, demolitions and poor weather. They had even used Greek fishing vessels and lighters to move stores along the Aegean coast.

In a fighting withdrawal the men of W Force held the Germans at Thermopylae on April 24. German air reconnaissance had confirmed that a defence line was under construction. On April 22 tanks and vehicles from the 5th Panzer Division, part of the XVIII Corps under General Böhme, attempted to bounce the Thermopylae position but were halted by fire from well camouflaged artillery and single tanks. The following day men of the German 6th *Gebirgsjäger* Division outflanked the position by working their way through difficult terrain to the west in conjunction with another outflanking manoeuvre through Molos. At Molos they

encountered strong resistance but on the night of April 24 – 25 W Force withdrew from the Thermopylae position.

This action and the access to ULTRA decrypts allowed the British to second guess the German moves and, in Operation *Demon*, evacuate not only many of their men, but also King George II of Greece, who flew out to Crete. *Luftwaffe* reports said that British troops were being evacuated from Salamis, and 20 large and 15 small ships were in the Athenian port of Piraeus and four large and 31 smaller vessels in Khalkis. All the ports were reported to be well protected by AA batteries.

At the Corinth Canal on April 25 German paratroopers were tasked with seizing the bridge that spanned the deep ship canal dividing the North and South Peloponnese. If the Germans could hold it they would speed the advance of the XII Army and also cut off the retreat of British and Commonwealth forces. The troops assigned to the task were

BELOW: The exhausted crew of a Bf110 heavy fighter rest as it is refuelled. The fighter had proved a disaster in the Battle of Britain but was effective in Greece.

RIGHT: Dornier Do17Z bombers fly in close formation over the Acropolis in central Athens following its capture on April 27, 1941. With a crew of four or five, the bomber had a maximum payload of 1,000kg (2,205lb) and a range of 1,500km (932 miles).

commanded by Colonel Sturm and consisted of 52 parachute engineers (*Fallschirmpioniere*) under Leutnant Häffner supported by the 1st and 2nd Battalions of *Fallschirmjäger* Regiment 2 (FJR 2) under respectively *Hauptmann* Kroh and *Hauptmann* Pietzonka with signals and medical detachments. It would be a classic attack with Kroh's battalion landing to the north of the bridge and Pietzonka's to the south. The engineers would then move in to remove any demolition charges that might be in place.

The force of 270 Ju52s took off from Larissa at 05.00 and the gliders carrying the engineers landed accurately at 07.00 with the engineers racing to capture the bridge. They

BREN LIGHT MACHINE-GUN

The Bren Light Machine Gun (LMG) initially built at the Royal Small Arms Factory at Enfield was based on the ZB 26, a LMG design from the Czechoslovakian small arms factory at Brno. The first two letters of the two names were combined to produce the "Bren", the versatile LMG that soldiered from World War II to the Gulf in 1991. The Bren was an air-cooled gas-operated weapon that fired a .303in (7.7mm) round from a 30-round box magazine. It had a slow rate of fire – 500rpm, but was very accurate, with sights set out to 1,829 metres (2,000yd), and light – it weighed only 9.95kg (22.12lb) and was 1,155mm (45.5in) long. It was easy to strip and experienced gunners could change magazines or barrels in less than five seconds. Brens were also made in Australia, Canada and India during the course of the war.

held it but were strongly counter-attacked and the situation was only resolved by the late arrival of the 2nd Battalion.

There are indications that ULTRA intercepts may have alerted the British troops at the bridge, however there is no explanation for what happened a few moments later. The engineers had removed the charges but moments later the bridge crashed down into the canal, possibly the structure was weakened and collapsed under the impact of a stray shell.

German losses were light, only eight engineers were killed, and a temporary structure was built across the canal by the morning of April 28. The capture of the Corinth Canal cut off the rearguard of the 4th New Zealand Brigade at Erithrae, but they were eventually evacuated from Port Raphti.

German forces reached Athens on April 27 and the German love affair with ancient Greece was given a new character as propaganda company photographers recorded the moment the *Reichskriegsflagge* was run up on

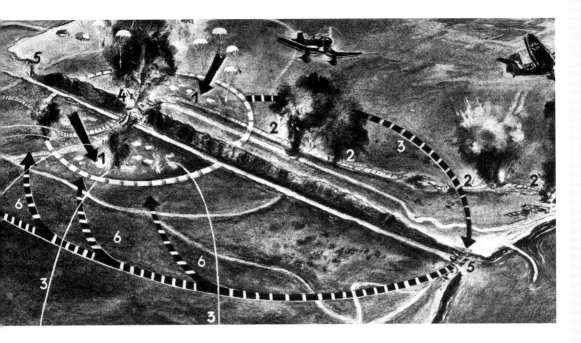

ABOVE: A dramatic reconstruction of the Corinth canal operation in the magazine *Signal*. It was published in 1944 as a morale booster when Germany was close to defeat.

BELOW: German artillerymen urge their horses across a river in Greece. Tanks and motorcycles might spearhead the attacks, but not all the German army was mechanised.

TOP: An officer salutes as the *Reichskriegsflagge* is raised on the Acropolis in Athens. The Germans saw themselves as ejecting the British from Greece, not as occupiers.

ABOVE: A Royal Navy submarine enters Port Said with the battleship HMS *Resolution* in the background. The battleship survived the war and was scrapped at Faslane in 1948.

a flagstaff on the Acropolis. In an act of symbolic resistance it would be torn down on the night of May 30–31, 1941 – one of the first of many acts of active and passive resistance during the occupation.

The campaign in Greece and Yugoslavia was a triumph for the German tactics of coordinating tanks, mechanised infantry and dive-bombers.

By April 28 W Force had been evacuated. For the operation the Royal Navy had provided six cruisers and 19 destroyers as well as numerous transports. Two destroyers and four transports were sunk and the bulk of troops evacuated to Crete.

ABOVE: An SdKfz 231 armoured car with a 2cm KwK cannon and 7.92mm MG passes the Greek parliament building in Athens following the surrender.

German casualties were 2,559 killed, 5,820 wounded and 3,169 missing. The British who had committed 75,000 to the campaign lost 12,000 men and all their heavy equipment. Some 6,298 Yugoslav officers and 337,864 NCOs and soldiers of Serbian extraction were taken prisoner. The Germans released Slovenian, Croatian and Macedonian prisoners. The Greeks, who were fully mobilised, lost 223,000 men.

UNTERNEHMEN MERKUR

Auf Kreta im Sturm und im Regen,

Da steht ein Fallschirmjäger auf der Wacht,

Er träumt ja so gerne von der Heimat,

Wo ihm ein holdes Mächenherze lacht.

Die Sternlein funkeln vom Himmel in die Nacht,

Grüß mir die Heimat,

Grüß mir mein Mägdelein aus blut'ger Schlacht.

'Auf Kreta im Sturm und im Regen'

– 'To Crete in storms and in rain' –

Fallschirmjäger song

The final stage in the German occupation of Greece, the attack on Crete between May 20-23, 1941, code named *Unternehmen Merkur* – Undertaking Mercury – was a unique battle.

On April 25 Hitler issued Directive No 28 stating that: "As a base for air warfare against Great Britain in the Eastern Mediterranean we must prepare to occupy the island of Crete."

The island was defended by 28,000 British and Commonwealth forces commanded by

General Bernard Freyberg, but many had been evacuated from the Greek mainland and had limited weapons, ammunition, transport and poor communications equipment.

For the capture of the island of Crete the Germans committed 13,000 paratroops of the 7th Air Division under Leutnant-General Kurt Student and 9,000 men of the 5th *Gebirgsjäger* Division under Major-General Julius Ringel with Colonel-General Alexander Lohr in overall command. They were supported by 500 fighters and bombers, 500 transports and 80 gliders.

The first air attacks on the island began on May 15 and in the light of the *Luftwaffe's* overwhelming superiority four days later

LEFT: General Freyberg enjoys a cigarette during a pause in the fighting in Crete. Despite enjoying the advantages of ULTRA his forces lacked the equipment and air support to defeat the Germans once they had gained a lodgement on the island.

ABOVE: Smoke rises from damaged or sunk ships in Suda Bay following German air attacks. The *Luftwaffe's* dominance of the air over Crete was critical for the operations by German paratroopers.

Freyberg ordered the remaining RAF aircraft to fly to Egypt. He assured Wavell that the airfields on the island would be rendered unusable. The daily attacks, known to the soldiers as the "Morning Hate", reached a crescendo just before 06.00 on May 20 when they concentrated on the AA gun positions as well as any identified infantry positions. At Maleme all but one of the AA guns was silenced: "This went on firing for some time," recalled a survivor, "till a host of Stukas and Me 109s fastened on it and shot and blasted it out of existence".

The island was held by 28,000 Imperial troops reinforced by Greek battalions and Cretan irregulars who brought the total

Continued on page 50.

LUFTWAFFE

The *Luftwaffe* was formally established in March 1935, however Germany had managed to develop medium range bombers and transports and train pilots from as early as 1926 in the state-subsidised airline *Deutsche Luft Hansa* (changed in 1934 to *Lufthansa*). Headed by Erhard Milch, a World War I veteran of both the infantry and air force, the civil airline operated the versatile Ju52 as well as sleek Heinkel airliners which were later re-engineered as bombers.

The Government sponsored the German Union of Sport Flying which by 1929 had 50,000 members. The organisation gave boys and young men the chance to fly gliders and light aircraft and provided an excellent pool of experienced or semi-trained pilots.

By the time Germany sided with Franco in the Spanish Civil War the *Luftwaffe* was well established and the war gave the pilots in the *Kondor Legion* the opportunity to test tactics and polish up flying skills as well as being valuable proving ground for aircraft. The Heinkel He111, Dornier Do17, Junkers Ju52, Ju87 and Ju88 and the Messerschmitt Bf109 and Bf110 were flown in action in Spain by pilots and crews who were rotated through the war zone. The *Kondor Legion* demonstrated to the awed world the effectiveness of air power when in July 1936 shuttles of Ju52s flew 7,350 Nationalist troops with their artillery and equipment from Morocco to Spain.

ORGANISATION OF XI AIR CORPS

First Wave
Group West
Major General Eugen Meindl
Assault Regiment
2 Coys 1st Bn (3 + 4)
2nd, 3rd, 4th Bns
1 Coy MG Bn

Group Centre
Lt General Wilhelm Süssmann
3rd Parachute Rgt (FJR 3)
2 Coys 1st Bn Assault Rgt (1 + 2)
MG Bn 1 Coy
Engineer Bn
Artillery, Anti-tank, Signals dets
100th Mountain Inf Rgt

Second Wave
Group Centre
Süssmann
2nd Parachute Rgt-2nd Bn
Support Dets

Group East
General Julius Ringel
1st Parachute Rgt (FJR 1)
2nd Parachute Bn (FJR 2)
5th Mountain Division - 100th Rgt
Reinforced M/C Bn
2nd Bn Panzer Rgt 31
Light Flak Bn

RIGHT: A promotional advertisement by the German company Dornier-Werke for its Do215 medium bomber. The detail shows the defensive machine gun positions around the cockpit.

Das Kampfflugzeug

DORNIER DO 215

verbindet hervorragende Flugeigenschaften mit hoher Kampfkraft. — Die Anordnung der Waffen gewährleistet beste Schußfelder nach allen Richtungen

Die geräumige Vollsichtkanzel nimmt die gesamte 4-köpfige Besatzung auf, die in Flug und Kampf ideal zusammen arbeiten kann

DORNIER-WERKE

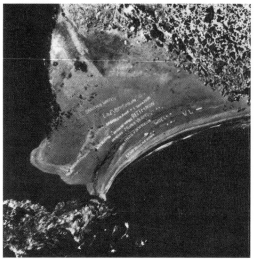

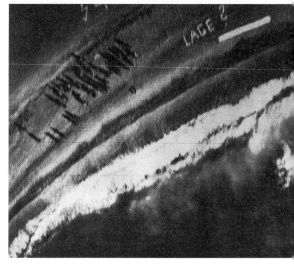

TOP: Wrecked tankers in Suda Bay. The superb natural anchorage and port facilities in the northwest corner of the island was an obvious target for air attacks and paratroop landings.

ABOVE LEFT AND RIGHT: Paratroops trapped on the beach near Retimo lay out ground to air signals for the *Luftwaffe*. Some 500 men of Group Centre survived the initial landings at Retimo.

ABOVE: The sky over Crete fills with parachutes. For the defenders the attack seemed almost futuristic, but the paratroops were terribly vulnerable in the air.

LEFT: Paratroops jump from Ju52s. Delays in take-offs later led to single aircraft flying over drop zones and bearing the brunt of heavy AA and small arms fire.

2ND LIEUTENANT CHARLES UPHAM, VC AND BAR

A modest 33-year-old New Zealand sheep farmer, "Charlie" Upham was awarded the Victoria Cross for his courage and leadership on Crete. On the night of May 21-22 he helped silence a German machine gun position. Between May 22–30, though wounded by two mortar bombs and a bullet through his foot, and suffering from dysentery, he continued to lead his platoon.

In 1942, promoted to Captain and now fighting in North Africa at El Ruweisat Ridge near El Alamein, he led his men in an attack that destroyed a German tank and several machine gun positions. He was captured and remained a PoW until 1945. For this action he received the rare distinction of a bar to his VC.

ABOVE AND RIGHT: The death dives of Ju52s photographed by Lt Gordon Hope-Morley who had taken his camera to photograph Cretan flora on the day of the attack. The pilot of the Ju52 manages to keep flying long enough for the men to jump over Heraklion.

garrison strength up to 42,500. Though the Allied forces were very poorly equipped they had a unique asset. ULTRA decrypts had given their commander Major General Bernard Freyberg VC, appointed on May 5, a complete breakdown of the German plans.

He knew where the proposed drop zones were located in Crete. However, Freyberg was under orders not to compromise his ULTRA intelligence by exactly second guessing the German moves and as a cover also positioned troops on the coast. He was aware that seaborne reinforcements were part of the German plan but, though concerned to reinforce the Maleme airfield area, he was overruled.

The island garrison lacked sufficient radios and so headquarters had to rely on runners, dispatch riders and field telephones – all

vulnerable to air attack. There were few tanks and these were battered veterans of the fighting in North Africa. Artillery consisted in part of captured Italian guns for which sights had been improvised with match sticks and chewing gum. The soldiers even lacked digging tools and were obliged to use their helmets to construct positions.

Operation *Merkur* divided the island into four drop zones: from west to east, Maleme,

Canea, Retimo and Heraklion. For lack of sufficient transport aircraft the island was attacked in two waves in the morning and the afternoon of May 20. Some 500 tough, reliable Ju52 transport aircraft were available in the XI Air Corps commanded by *Generalmajor* Conrad. The Corps consisted of *Geschwader* 1, 2 and 3, making up ten transport groups. They would fly from airfields at Tanagra, Topolis, Dadion, Megara, Corinth, Phaleron and Elevsis.

The first wave, Group West under *Generalmajor* Eugen Meindl, would land in Maleme/Canea zone. They would be spearheaded by the 1st Assault Regiment in DFS230 gliders who would land to the west of Maleme airfield and around Suda Bay to neutralise any AA guns that had survived the air attacks. This would prepare the way for the paratroops.

ABOVE: With the fighting over a *Luftwaffe* motorcycle crew gaze at a crash-landed Ju52, the port engine of which has been ripped from its mountings. This is probably Maleme airfield.

ABOVE RIGHT: Men of the 5th Mountain Division wait at airfields near Athens, ready for the flight across the Aegean. Commanded by the bearded Austrian General Julius Ringel, the division composed of the 85th and 100th Mountain Regiments proved critical in the battle for Crete.

RIGHT: Some men are pensive and others joke nervously as, wearing life jackets, *Gebirgsjäger*, sit rifle in hand, in the bucket seats of their Ju52 as it roars across the sea. Upon landing the drill was to exit the aircraft as quickly as possible.

GREEK SACRED REGIMENT

This special forces unit was formed in August 1942 from officers of the Royal Hellenic Army who had escaped to Egypt. About 300 enlisted as soldiers and it was the only Greek unit to be regularly employed operationally. It was the regiment's third incarnation, having been first formed in 370BC and then again in 1821 during Greece's fight for freedom. The Regiment became part of the SAS and took part in the campaign in North Africa in 1943. It was attached to the SBS and conducted operations in the Aegean. It also assisted British forces to quell the Communist ELAS rising in Athens in December 1944.

In the afternoon, Group Centre under *Generalmajor* Süssmann would land at Retimo and Canea/Suda, and Group East under *Generalleutnant* Julius Ringel, spearheaded by paratroops of FJR 1 and a battalion of FJR 2, would seize the airfield at Heraklion. This would allow the bulk of the 5th *Gebirgsjäger* Division to be flown in by Ju 52s.

Bad luck dogged the Germans from the outset of the attack. The glider carrying *Generalmajor* Wilhelm Süssmann crashed on an island off the Greek mainland and Major General Meindl was critically wounded shortly after landing. The Germans had also underestimated the physical difficulties of

ABOVE AND BELOW: A mopping up operation in Crete. Paratroops move cautiously through an olive grove before throwing stick grenades into a British position and launching an attack. Many Australian and New Zealand troops were captured as they fought rearguard actions that allowed British troops to be evacuated by the Royal Navy from the tiny southern harbour at Sphakia.

ABOVE: British soldiers emerge to surrender following the attack by the paratroops armed with Kar 98K rifles. Paratroops were also armed with the MP38 submachine gun and MG34 machine gun.

LEFT: A sniper, distinctive by his goggles, takes weapons from a *Waffenbehälter* – Weapon's Container. A platoon of 40 to 50 paratroops required 14 containers that were painted with distinguishing coloured bands.

fighting in Crete and the size and determination of the garrison. The olive groves provided excellent camouflage for the defenders and the terraced hillsides reduced much of the effect of bombing.

The German airborne attack philosophy was to jump directly onto the objective – even though this ran the risk of incurring heavy casualties. The British and American approach was to have a safe DZ away from the objective and so allow the paratroopers to form into a cohesive group – however, this ran the risk that the force would be intercepted before it reached its objective.

When they jumped the men were lightly armed and had to collect heavier weapons from containers that were parachuted with them. In the short time that men were in the air on their parachutes they were easy targets for riflemen below. On the ground the British

ABOVE: A Junkers Ju88 dive bomber roars low across the sea in an anti-shipping strike against ships off Crete. The Royal Navy lost cruisers and destroyers in these attacks but evacuated 16,500 men.

and Anzac troops quickly established the most effective technique was to aim at the paratrooper's feet as he descended. One defender described it as being "like the opening of the duck shooting season in New Zealand".

The gliders came in so low and slow that the defenders could fire right into them killing all the occupants before they had even hit the ground. Even those that landed with the soldiers still alive hit rocky, terraced terrain and broke up, killing or injuring the occupants.

Paratroops who landed at the little fishing port of Kastelli west of Maleme were killed

ABOVE: A paratroop pioneer sprints forward moments after firing a burst with his M1941 Kleif flamethrower. The flamethrower was a very effective weapon against bunkers, but it was heavy, bulky and short ranged.

LEFT: Fatigued and shocked paratroops describe the heavy fighting that proved so costly to General Student. Though the losses in Crete were made up Hitler was convinced that "the day of the paratrooper is over".

RIGHT: Shells explode a few metres away from *Fallschirmjäger* as they take cover from British artillery fire. The paratroops may have lacked artillery but they had dive bombers on call.

by Cretan irregulars, men dressed in the traditional costume of baggy black trousers and high boots. Armed with knives, axes and hunting rifles they attacked these airborne enemies. When Crete was finally occupied the Germans shot 200 men from Kastelli for these "atrocities".

In the afternoon the second wave flew into disaster. In just one hour a force of 1,500 *Fallschirmjäger* was reduced to 1,000 men in small scattered groups being hunted and trapped. At Retimo, Group Centre in the second wave was trapped in an olive factory, under siege by the British and Australian forces. Dust now shrouded the airfields in Greece and in the chaos the *Luftwaffe* released aircraft that arrived at Heraklion in relays and so were easy targets for the well camouflaged defenders. On the morning of May 21 Piper Macpherson of the Black Watch climbed out of his slit trench at Heraklion and sounded reveille – the British and Anzac

troops with their Cretan allies were confident almost cocky.

By the end of the day 40 per cent of Student's assault force was either dead, wounded or a prisoner. "Today has been a hard one," Freyberg cabled Wavell in Egypt. "We have been hard pressed. So far, I believe, we hold aerodromes at Heraklion and Maleme...Margin by which we hold them is a bare one, and it would be wrong of me to paint an optimistic picture. Fighting has been heavy and we have killed large numbers of Germans. Communications are most difficult".

Only at the western end of Maleme airfield did the paratroops manage to find cover and set up a viable base in the dried up riverbed of the Tavronitis.

The key feature that dominated the airfield was the hill known as Point 107 that was held by the New Zealand 22nd Battalion commanded by Lt Colonel Les Andrew.

MAX SCHMELING BOXER AND PARATROOPER

In World War II Max Schmeling, the German heavyweight boxing champion, enlisted in the *Fallschirmjäger*. The Nazi propaganda machine made much of him during his parachute training. In May 1941, though ill from eating fresh fruit in mainland Greece, he jumped into action in Crete. It was reported that he had been hospitalised and in Berlin Goering assumed he had been wounded and ordered that he should be awarded the EK II (Iron Cross Second Class). In reality he was still ill with diarrhoea.

Under heavy air attack and enemy probes he sent runners to his commanding officer Brigadier James Hargest requesting assistance. Hargest promised a counter attack against the men in the Tavronitis but his men were pinned down by air attacks. Andrew attempted an attack with a tiny force of 40 men and two Matilda tanks but it failed, and only three men returned unwounded. A brave and experienced soldier, Andrew who had won the VC in World War I, was under intense pressure and without reliable communications. His battalion appeared to be in danger of being cut off so Andrew pulled back A Company on Point 107 and this gave the Germans their opening.

With an airfield in their possession, albeit under spasmodic artillery fire, they poured in reinforcements. On the first day aircraft landed 650 mountain troops and 550 more paratroops were landed. The Germans now prepared to "roll up" the island, pushing eastwards from their secure base at Maleme. In Athens Student took the tough but tactically sound decision to abandon the operations at Retimo and Heraklion. On May 20 1,500 and 2,000 men had been committed to these locations, and a day later only 120 men landed at Heraklion, while at the Maleme, Galatas and Suda Bay area 1,880 were parachuted in. On May 22 this figure jumped to 1,950 and on the 23rd the *Luftwaffe* landed 3,650 men. On May 25 Student landed at Maleme. The airfield was littered with smashed Ju52s and to those who knew him the General looked tired and aged. He had

LEFT: Max Schmeling, the German World heavyweight boxing champion who was a *Fallschirmjäger,* features on the cover of *Signal.* Though the Nazi propaganda ministry made much of Schmeling, he was a widely respected apolitical sportsman. He survived the war and still enjoys a vigorous lifestyle.

LEFT: A lone Ju52 flies low across Crete. The need to fly straight and level at low speed to allow paratroops to exit safely made all troop carrying aircraft desperately vulnerable to ground fire. Mix ups at the airfields in Greece meant that many aircraft in the second wave came in alone and not as part of a formation and so suffered heavily.

witnessed the destruction of his creation, the 7th Air Division.

On May 22 Freyberg decided that he would have to pull his forces back on Suda to secure the naval base. In five days of hard fighting the paratroops had reached the outskirts of Canea and Freyberg had to face the fact that the battle of Crete was lost. He signalled Wavell: "From a military point of view our position is hopeless," and on May 27 London gave permission to withdraw.

He organised an evacuation initially from the better appointed port of Heraklion on the north coast, but was eventually forced to use the tiny south coast port of Sphakia. To cover

these operations two Commandos commanded by Brigadier Robert Laycock and designated Layforce were landed at Suda Bay on the nights of May 23-24 and 26-27. Among their number was the writer Evelyn Waugh who was the formations intelligence officer. In his novel *Officers and Gentlemen* he described the fighting in Crete from an idiosyncratic and rather jaundiced viewpoint.

"The Navy has never let the Army down," signalled Admiral Sir Andrew Cunningham. "No enemy forces must reach Crete by sea." On the night of May 21-22 a Royal Navy force commanded by Rear Admiral Irvine Glennie acting on ULTRA intelligence intercepted a

MASCHINENPISTOLE MP38/40

The German *Maschinenpistole* MP38 and MP40 sub-machine guns, originally manufactured at the Erma-Werke at Erfurt, had several revolutionary features. No wood was used in their construction, only steel and plastic, and they had a folding metal butt ideal for paratroopers and armoured vehicle crews. The 9mm calibre MP38 and MP40 both fired from a 32-round box magazine with a distinctive cyclic rate of 500 rounds a minute. They were 833mm (32.6in) long with the butt extended and 630mm (24.8in) with it folded. Manufacturing changes to increase production reduced machining and replaced it with welding and steel pressings. This reduced the weight of the MP40 to 4.027kg (8.87lb), compared to 4.086kg (9lb) in the MP38.

convoy of 25 commandeered *caiques* – Greek fishing boats – escorted by the Italian destroyer *Lupo*. The Royal Navy sank several *caiques* and others turned back. They were carrying elements of the 5th *Gebirgsjäger* Division with their vehicles, Flak and support weapons, as well as engineer and anti-tank units. A larger group of 35 vessels intended to support Group East on the second day returned to Milos but some boats did make landfall on the island.

These attacks came at a cost, and on May 21 the Royal Navy had suffered its first casualties when at dawn German aircraft sank the destroyer HMS *Juno* and damaged the cruiser HMS *Ajax*. A day later the losses mounted as the cruisers HMS *Gloucester* and *Fiji* were

sunk along with the destroyer HMS *Greyhound*. *Gloucester* and *Greyhound* had been patrolling the Kithira Channel to the north-west of the island, on the look out for troop-carrying convoys. On May 23 the destroyers HMS *Kelly* and *Kashmir* were lost, the former captained by Lord Mountbatten. On May 29 the destroyers HMS *Imperial* and *Hereward* were sunk off the north coast.

For the men making the fighting withdrawal to the south, it was a grim slog across the mountain spine of the *Levka* (White) Mountains to Sphakia. The men at Retimo never received the order to withdraw and when German forces finally arrived in the area they found that 500 paratroops were virtual prisoners in the olive oil factory, surrounded

by 1,500 Australian and Greek troops. In the olive groves and fields lay the bodies of over 700 *Fallschirmjäger*.

At Retimo and Heraklion Australian and British forces had quickly learned how to confuse the *Luftwaffe* transports and bombers. They laid out captured swastika flags on their positions, stopped shooting when aircraft appeared and when the Germans fired green recognition flares, fired similar signals. On a number of occasions laying out captured recognition panels produced the prompt delivery of weapons, ammunition, rations and medical stores.

The evacuation of the garrison by the Royal Navy had been costly, but when it ended on June 1, 16,500 men had been saved.

ABOVE: This dramatic and very inaccurate map published in *Signal* shows the three drop zones and suggests that all were successful. In reality it was only at Maleme that the paratroopers gained a small toehold and eventually after hard fighting they secured the island.

Cunningham was an inspirational leader for his crews: "It takes the Navy three years to build a ship. It would take 300 years to rebuild a tradition."

However so severe were the losses at Crete that the Germans never attempted a major airborne operation again. Hitler declared to Student that: "the day of the paratrooper is over. The parachute arm is a surprise weapon and without the element of surprise there can

be no future for airborne forces," and with these words he condemned this superb force to a ground role. If it had been used against Malta or Cyprus this would have shifted the strategic balance in the Mediterranean firmly in favour of the Axis. Paratroops, were, however, used in some small scale operations in the latter years of the war, including the Aegean, and the Ardennes offensive in 1944-45.

Conquered Greece was divided among the Axis powers. Bulgaria took Western Thrace and so had access to the Aegean and after 1943 this area was expanded westwards into Macedonia. However Germany had control of the border with Turkey along with the offshore islands of Lemnos, Lesbos and Chios.

The bulk of Greece was administered by the Italians, with the exception of Athens, the port of Piraeus and the western two-thirds of Crete including Suda Bay. Following Italy's surrender in September 1943 German troops pushed into the whole of Greece.

By May 9, 1945, on the last day of the war, the Germans had evacuated Greece, but the garrison of western Crete was trapped

ABOVE: The fighting over, paratroops march down to the docks in Crete. Men were shocked to discover how heavy the losses were when they returned to almost empty barracks in Germany.

without shipping with which to reach the mainland. Along with the islands of Milos, Leros and Rhodes, they were grandly designated *Festungen* – fortresses.

The Balkan campaign, forced on the Germans by Italian adventurism in Greece in 1941, had delayed the attack on the USSR by a critical two months. It had been scheduled for May 15 but would be launched on June 22. The mud and snow of the winter of 1941 would not have stopped the Panzers outside Moscow, they would still have had eight weeks good going if they had attacked in May.

RIGHT: The air and sea battle over and around Crete saw the *Luftwaffe* pitched against the Royal Navy. Though the navy suffered heavy losses, it managed to evacuate many men from the island and intercept enemy convoys carrying troops and equipment to support the airborne landings.

LEFT: Dust shrouds an airfield where Ju52s are loaded and Bf110 fighters are refuelled and re-armed.

ABOVE: The *"Kreta"* cuff title awarded to troops who had landed or fought between May 20 and 27, or aircrew who had taken part in air operations.

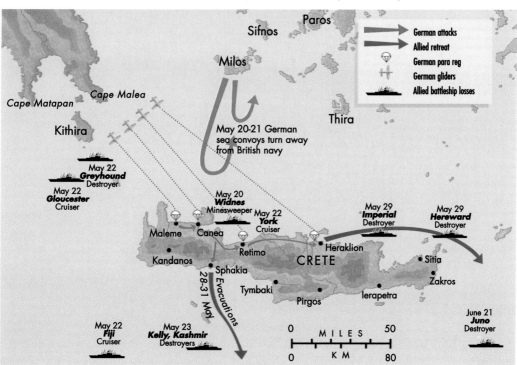

May 20-21 German sea convoys turn away from British navy

Paros
Sifnos
Milos
Thira

Cape Matapan Cape Malea
Kithira

May 22
Greyhound Destroyer
May 22
Gloucester Cruiser

May 20
Widnes Minesweeper
May 22
York Cruiser

Maleme Canea
Kandanos
Retimo
Sphakia
CRETE
Heraklion

May 29
Imperial Destroyer
May 29
Hereward Destroyer

Sitia
Zakros

Tymbaki
Pirgos
Ierapetra

28-31 May Evacuations

May 22
Fiji Cruiser
May 23
Kelly, Kashmir Destroyers

June 21
Juno Destroyer

German attacks
Allied retreat
German para reg
German gliders
Allied battleship losses

MILES
0   50
0   80
K M

AFRIKA KORPS ASCENDANT

Über die Schelde die Maas und den Rhein
stießen die Panzer nach Frankreich hinein.
Husaren des Führers im schwarzen Gewand,
so haben sie Frankreich im Sturm überrannt!
Es rasseln die Ketten, es dröhnt der Motor,
Panzer rollen in Afrika vor!
Panzer rollen in Afrika vor!

'Panzer rollen in Afrika vor!'
– 'Tanks roll forward in Africa' –

While the Balkans campaign was being fought out, on the other side of the Mediterranean Germany was again coming to the assistance of its unreliable ally. The Italians had been driven back deep into their colony of Libya by British and Commonwealth forces and so Berlin decided that a small number of troops should be sent to assist them. On Tuesday February 18, 1941, the force was designated the *Deutsches Afrika Korps* (DAK) or *Afrika Korps* and consisted of the 15th Panzer and 5th

ABOVE: General Erwin Rommel salutes the newly formed *Afrika Korps* in Tripoli on February 27, 1941.

Light (later renamed 21st Panzer) Divisions, though the title would be used for all German forces serving in North Africa from 1941 to 1943.

It was commanded by Lieutenant General Erwin Rommel, a soldier who would be as much respected by his British and Commonwealth enemies, who nicknamed him the "Desert Fox", as by the soldiers under his command. Rommel, who had served with distinction in World War I, commanded the *Afrika Korps* from February 18, 1941 to March 9, 1943, during which time he outfought the British and Commonwealth forces on numerous occasions.

Rommel was an aggressive and energetic leader and before his forces were fully up to strength he elected to attack. The first contact between the *Afrika Korps* and the men of Wavell's Middle East Command was by a

ABOVE: One of several propaganda pictures taken showing the arrival of the *Afrika Korps* in Libya. Rommel was quick to take the offensive against the over-extended British and Commonwealth forces.

ABOVE: A salute from the commander of an 8 x 8 SdKfz 231 heavy armoured car. It had a crew of four and was used for a variety of roles.

BLITZKRIEG

RIGHT: The commander of an SdKfz 250/3 of 3rd Battery 21 Panzer Division holds onto the frame antenna as the half track bucks through the desert sand.

BELOW: A BMW R75 motor cycle combination of the 21 Panzer Division churns through the desert. Heat, sand, grit and rocks played havoc with engines of tanks and trucks.

BELOW RIGHT: An SdKfz 250 is off loaded at docks in Libya. Axis convoys carrying men, equipment, fuel and ammunition were regularly intercepted by RAF aircraft and RN submarines.

PzKpfw IV Ausf F2

The PzKpfw IV was built under a 1934 specification from the Germany Army Weapons Department. It entered service in 1939 and was in production until 1945, with a total of 9,000 vehicles being built by Krupp. The same chassis was used for the Ausf F2 variant up-gunned and armoured tanks and despite the increase in weight the tank enjoyed good mobility and an excellent power-to-weight ratio. It was also used for a wide range of SP guns and other specialised armour.

Armament:	75mm (2.95in) L/43; 2 x 7.92mm MGs
Armour:	20mm-50mm (0.78in-1.96in)
Weight:	18,400kg (18.11 tons)
Hull length:	5.60m (18ft 4in)
Width:	2.90m (9ft 6in)
Height:	2.65m (8ft 7in)
Engine:	Maybach HL108TR, V-12, petrol, 250hp at 3,000rpm
Road speed:	31km/h (19mph)
Range:	170km (105 miles)

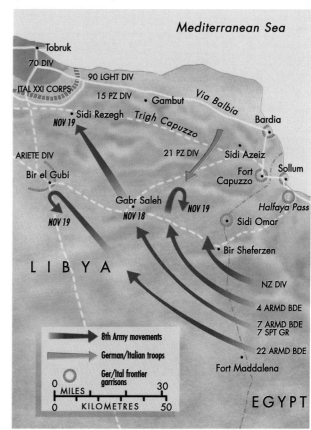

RIGHT: Operation *Crusader* was launched at 06.00 on November 18 1941 and caught Rommel and the *DAK* off balance. The attack took British and Commonwealth troops back into Libya and lifted the siege of Tobruk. However, the ever resourceful Rommel bounced back in January 1942. Now it was the British 8th Army that was in retreat.

ABOVE: The US tanker *Ohio* limps into the Grand Harbour at Valletta, Malta after surviving the Pedestal convoy in August 1942. She delivered 10,000 tons of fuel to the island.

RIGHT: A British soldier emerges from a knocked out Mk III Valentine tank. The Valentine was armed with a 2-Pdr gun and a machine gun.

reconnaissance patrol on February 24 at Nofilia on the Libyan coast. The Germans then hit the British positions at Al Agheila on March 24, 1941 and as the exhausted British forces fell back this allowed the DAK to roam deep into the desert. The British 2nd Armoured Division at Mersa Brega fought for a day on March 31 but was forced back. Benghazi fell on April 4, Derna on the 7th and Rommel had driven the British out of Halfaya Pass and crossed the Egyptian border by April 25.

The Italian and German forces lacked the strength to take the port of Tobruk that was cut off on April 10. It held for six months deep behind Axis lines, garrisoned by men of the 9th Australian Division under General Morshead and supplied at night by sea. Between August 19 - 29 the Australians were replaced by Polish troops. They were helped by ULTRA intelligence that gave them advanced warning of where and when the Germans would attack.

On May 12 a convoy, code named Tiger, arrived at Alexandria carrying urgently needed tanks and aircraft for the British. At considerable risk it had been sent through the Mediterranean rather than by the longer safer route around the Cape. The *Afrika Korps* survived two operations mounted by General Wavell *Brevity* on May 15 that recaptured Halfaya Pass, Sollum and Capuzzo and *Battleaxe* on June 15. The Germans believed that both operations were attempts to relieve Tobruk.

Wavell's successor General Claude Auchinleck, commanding an enlarged British and Commonwealth force renamed the 8th Army, launched Operation *Crusader* at 06.00 on November 18, 1941. The 8th Army now had over 700 tanks while the *Afrika Korps*

BELOW: A battery of *Afrika Korps* heavy 15cm K18 guns in action. The gun weighed 12,460kg (27,412lbs) in action and had a maximum range of 24,825m (27,060yds).

M3A1 STUART MK III

The American M3 Light, known to the British as the Stuart or to press and propagandists as the "Honey", was a fast mechanically reliable light tank. It entered production in the USA in 1941 and some 6,000 were built and operated with the Red Army as well as British and US forces. Its drawback was its thin armour that made it very vulnerable and consequently unpopular with its crews.

Armament:	One 37mm (1.46in) M6 gun, three 0.30in (7.62mm) MGs
Armour:	51mm (2in)
Crew:	4
Dimensions:	Length 4.54m (14ft 10in); Width 2.22m (7ft 4in); Height 2.3m (7ft 7in)
Weight:	12,927kg (12.7 tons)
Powerplant:	Continental W-670, 7-cylinder, radial, petrol, 250hp (186.6kW)
Speed:	58km/h (36mph)
Range:	**113km (70 miles)**

MEDIUM TANK M3 (LEE/GRANT MK I)

Developed in the USA in the light of combat experience in France and North Africa the M3 Medium, known to the British as the Grant, reflected the realisation that tanks needed more powerful armament. A 75mm gun with limited traverse was mounted in the hull and a smaller turret-mounted 35mm gun was addec. This gave the vehicle a high silhouette. Despite this it was mechanically reliable and welcomed by British crews in North Africa when it performed well against *Afrika Korps* tanks in May 1942.

Armament:	One 75mm (2.95in) M2 or M3 cannon, one 37mm (1.46in) M5 or M6 cannon, four 0.30in (7.62mm) MGs
Armour:	57mm (2.24in)
Crew:	6
Dimensions:	Length 5.64m (18ft 6in); Width 2.72m (8ft 11in); Height 3.12m (10ft 3in)
Weight:	27,216kg (26.7 tons)
Powerplant:	Continental, R-975-EC2 or E1, radial, petrol, 340hp (253.5 kW)
Speed:	42km/h (26mph)
Range:	193km (120 miles)

Mk VI light tank (1936)

Light tanks had been developed from the 1930s based on the Carden-Loyd tankette concept and the Mk VI was the second British tank of this type to have a three man crew. It saw action in France, the Balkans and North Africa. Though it was agile and fairly reliable, the armour was thin and armament light. After 1942 the light tanks were withdrawn and replaced by Stuarts. Surviving vehicles were used for training.

Armament:	One 7.7mm (0.303in) MG; one 12.75mm (0.50in) MG
Armour:	4mm to 14mm (0.25in to 0.65in)
Crew:	3
Dimensions:	Length 4.01m (13ft 2in); Width 2.08m (6ft 10in); Height 2.26m (7ft 5in)
Weight:	4,875kg (4.8 tons)
Powerplant:	Meadows 6-cylinder petrol 65.6kW (88bhp)
Speed:	56km/h (35mph)
Range:	200km (125 miles)

M4 (early Sherman)

Using the same hull and suspension as the M3 Medium tank the Americans produced a tank that, though less well armoured than other designs and prone to catch fire when hit, it became a war winner simply by dint of the numbers that were built. When production ceased in 1945 factories had made 40,000. The hull was used for many variants including a mine clearing tank, bridge layer, recovery vehicle and rocket launcher. It would soldier on after the war, upgunned and with modified suspension into the late 1960s.

Armament:	One 75mm (2.95in) gun, one 0.5in (12.7mm) MG, two 0.30in (7.62mm) MGs
Armour:	62mm (2.44in)
Crew:	5
Dimensions:	Length 5.88m (19ft 4in); Width 2.68m (8ft 7in); Height 2.74m (9m)
Weight:	33,180kg (32.66 tons)
Powerplant:	Wright R-975-C1, radial, 9-cylinder, 298kW (400hp)
Speed:	39km/h (24mph)
Range:	160km (100 miles)

BIRTH OF THE SAS

"To: The Commander-in-Chief, Middle East Forces

From: Lieutenant D. Stirling, 8 Commando

Subject: A Special Service Unit

a The enemy is exceedingly vulnerable to attack along the line of his coastal communications and various transport parks, aerodromes and other targets strung out along the coast. The role of 8 Commando which has attempted raids on these targets is most vulnerable.

b The scale on which the Commando raids are planned, i.e. the number of troops employed on the one hand and the scale of equipment and facilities on the other, prejudices surprise beyond all possible compensating advantages in respect of the defensive and aggressive striking power afforded. Moreover, the Navy has to provide to lift the force which results in the risking of naval units valuable out of all proportion even to a successful raid.

c There is great advantage to be gained in establishing a Special Service unit based on the principle of the fullest exploitation of surprise and of making the minimum demands on manpower and equipment. The application of this principle will mean, in effect, the employment of a small sub-unit to cover a target previously requiring 4 or 5 troops of a Commando, i.e. about 200 men. If an aerodrome or transport park is the objective of an operation, then the destruction of 50 aircraft or units of transport will be more easily accomplished by just one of my proposed sub-units than a force of 200 men. It follows that 200 properly selected, trained and equipped men, organised into

these sub-units, will be able to attack up to 10 different objectives at the same time on the same night as compared to only one objective using the current Commando technique. So, only 25% success in the former is equivalent to many times the maximum result in the latter.

d The corollary of this is that a unit operating on these principles will have to be so trained as to be capable of arriving on the scene of operation by every practicable method, by land, sea or air; and furthermore the facilities for the lift must not be of a type valuable in tactical scale operations. If in any particular operation a sub-unit is to be parachuted it will be from an aircraft conveniently available without any modifications; if by sea, then the sub-unit will be transported either by submarine or caiques, and trained in the use of folboats (a six foot long, two man collapsible canoe made of a wooden frame with rubberised canvas cover); if by land, the unit will be trained either to infiltrate on foot or be carried within 10 or 15 miles of the target by another experienced unit.

e The unit must be responsible for its own training and operational planning and therefore the Commander of the Unit must operate directly under the order of the Commander-in-Chief. It would be fatal for the proposed unit to be put under any existing branch or formation for administration. The head of any such branch or formation would be less experienced than me or my successor in the strategic medium in which it is proposed to operate.

f It is no secret that an offensive is being planned for November 1941. Attached is my plan for the use of the unit in that offensive.

PLAN FOR THE NOVEMBER OFFENSIVE

"1 Target: Enemy fighter and bomber landing grounds at TMIMI and GAZALA.

2 Method: In the night of D minus 2, 5 sections to be parachuted on to drop zones some 12 miles south of the objectives; this will preserve surprise. Each section is of 12 men (i.e. 3 sub-sections of 4). As cover a heavy raid is required on GAZALA and TMIMI using as many flares as possible to aid navigation to the drop zones.

3 After re-assembly on the drop zones each section will spend the balance of the night D minus 2 in getting to pre-arranged lying-up points from which they will observe the targets the next day. The following night (D minus 1) each party will carry out its raid so as to arrive on the target at the same time.

4 Each party will carry a total of about 60 incendiary-cum-explosive bombs equipped with 2-hour, ½-hour and 10-minute time pencils in addition to a 12-second fuse. The time pencils will be used on a time de-escalating basis to ensure almost simultaneous detonation.

5 After the raid each party will retire independently into the desert to a prearranged meeting place south of the TRIG EL ABD to rendezvous with a patrol of the Long Range Desert Group."

were reduced to 320 tanks of which nearly half were Italian. The attack initially achieved complete surprise but Rommel's quick reactions nearly destroyed the British plan. On November 24 Rommel ordered his tanks to thrust eastwards to cut off the 8th Army. This panicked General Cunningham who wanted to call off the offensive. Auchinleck overrode him and replaced him by his Deputy Chief of Staff General Neil Ritchie. By now Rommel was low on fuel and on December 4 the 8th Army punched through to relieve Tobruk as the *Afrika Korps* withdrew to Gazala. On January 17 Bardia was recaptured by the British. By now both sides were exhausted. The Axis had suffered 30,000 casualties and the 8th Army

RIGHT: A wounded French survivor of the fighting at Bir Hacheim waits for evacuation by air. Normally lightly wounded would be carried in ambulances or trucks.

ABOVE: A PzKpfw IV drives past a captured 8th Army Bren Gun Carrier. The *Afrika Korps* made extensive use of captured vehicles, equipment and even artillery.

BELOW: Rommel's counter thrust in 1942 that took him deep into Egypt. In Cairo and Alexandria nervous British officials and staff officers began burning classified documents.

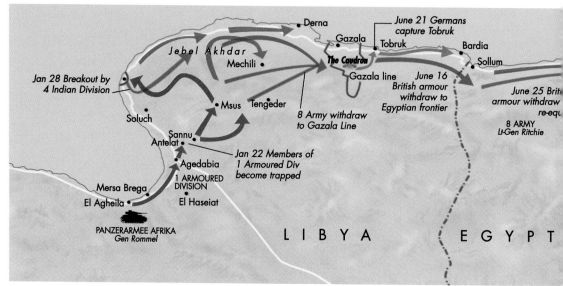

Jebel Akhdar

Derna

Gazala

Tobruk — June 21 Germans capture Tobruk

Bardia

Sollum

Mechili

The Cauldron

Gazala line

June 16 British armour withdraw to Egyptian frontier

Jan 28 Breakout by 4 Indian Division

Msus

Tengeder

8 Army withdraw to Gazala Line

June 25 Brit armour withdraw re-equ

Soluch

Sannu

Antelat

Jan 22 Members of 1 Armoured Div become trapped

8 ARMY
Lt-Gen Ritchie

Agedabia

1 ARMOURED DIVISION

Mersa Brega

El Agheila

El Haseiat

PANZERARMEE AFRIKA
Gen Rommel

L I B Y A

E G Y P T

LEFT: An *Afrika Korps* MG34 crew in a rocky emplacement. The Western Desert included rocks as well as sand.

ABOVE: Rommel with Hauptmann Dr *"Pappa"* Willi Bach and *Afrika Korps* staff at Sollum. Bach, a former Pastor commanding 1st Bn If Rgt 104, though cut off, had held Halfaya Pass until relieved by 15th Panzer Div on July 17, 1941. For this spirited defence Bach was awarded the Knight's Cross.

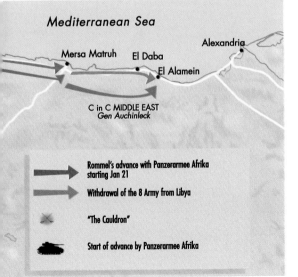

Mediterranean Sea

Alexandria

Mersa Matruh　El Daba

El Alamein

C in C MIDDLE EAST
Gen Auchinleck

Rommel's advance with Panzerarmee Afrika starting Jan 21

Withdrawal of the 8 Army from Libya

"The Cauldron"

Start of advance by Panzerarmee Afrika

18,000 and each side had lost 300 tanks.

As part of Operation *Crusader*, on the night of November 17 – 18 the first operation of the Special Air Service was launched to attack *Luftwaffe* bases. It was a failure but the operation marks the origins of the British Army's élite special forces regiment. Earlier David Stirling, the youthful commander of the formation, had mapped out the regiment's role in a memorandum presented to Generals Auchinleck and Ritchie. The 24-year-old Scots Guards officer, who had served with Layforce, was given permission to raise and train a force of 60 men.

Stirling had provisionally named the force 62 Commando but was told that it would be called L Detachment Special Air Service (SAS) Brigade. The title SAS Brigade was chosen in order to convince German intelligence that the 8th Army had an airborne force in the theatre.

The 1st SAS Brigade had been created as a "ghost" unit by Lt Col Dudley Clarke. With two officers and ten other ranks Clarke commanded "Advanced HQ 'A' Force" which was a strategic deception organisation. The idea for the airborne unit had been developed following the battle of Sidi Barrani in December 1940 when the captured diary of an Italian officer had revealed fears that the British paratroops might land behind Axis lines.

The distinctive cap badge, motto "Who Dares Wins" and parachute wings were

ABOVE RIGHT: *Afrika Korps* engineers make the final checks on a bridge across the anti-tank ditch that protected Tobruk. The Italian-built defences for the port were well constructed.

RIGHT: Sunken ships and wrecked vehicles at Tobruk harbour after it had been captured by the *Afrika Korps*. The Germans also secured huge stocks of food and fuel.

HANS-JOACHIM MARSEILLE
(1909 – 1942)

German fighter ace who, with 158 kills, ranked number 29. Significantly these were against experienced British and Commonwealth pilots in the Western Desert – even after his death he remained the top scoring German ace in the West. Nicknamed the "Star of Africa" his untidy good looks and bohemian style made him almost as popular as a singer or film star with women in Germany. He was killed when his Me Bf109 caught fire and his parachute malfunctioned when he bailed out. He was awarded the Knight's Cross with Oak Leaves, Swords and Diamonds.

FIESELER FI156C-2 *STORCH* (STORK)

The Storch entered service in 1937 and served throughout the war as a liaison aircraft and air ambulance. It had a very low stalling speed that allowed it to virtually hover, while its short take-off and landing capability made it superb in cramped landing grounds. About 40 captured aircraft were used by the Allies and during the war Germany and subsidiary factories in occupied Europe produced 2,549 aircraft.

Type:	Army co-operation/liaison
Crew:	2
Power Plant:	One 240hp Argus As 10C
Performance:	Maximum speed at sea level 175km/h (109mph)
Normal range:	385km (239 miles)
Weights:	Empty 930kg (2,050lb) Loaded 1,320kg (2,910lb)
Dimensions:	Wing span 14.25m (46ft 9in) Length: 9.90m (32ft 5in) Height: 3.05m (10ft 0in)
Armament:	One 7.92mm MG15 in rear cockpit glazing.

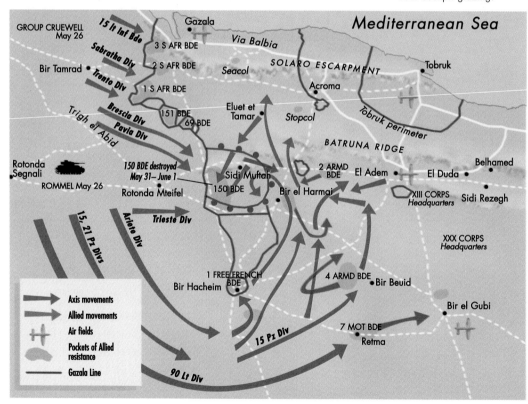

ABOVE: A Storch lifts off from a rough airstrip. It was used for observation and liaison work.

devised by members of the SAS during moments of leisure in Egypt. What was entertaining for them was very useful for Clarke since reports of an airborne unit in Egypt were picked up by agents working for the Germans.

The SAS would develop raiding techniques against Axis airfields that would destroy more than 250 aircraft on the ground, more than the RAF achieved in the air. Among the targets were the invaluable Ju52 transport aircraft. Rommel said of the SAS that it "caused us more damage than any other

LEFT: The dramatic manoeuvre that took *Panzerarmee Afrika* around the 8th Army defences and into the Battle of Knightsbridge on June 13-18, 1942.

RIGHT: An Italian soldier of the *Bersaglieri* guards British prisoners.

British unit of equal strength".

On January 21 Rommel attacked and the 21st Panzer Division seized Mersa Brega while 15th Panzer to its south advanced to Wadi Faregh and swung north to Agedadia. The British were taken by surprise and on January 22 they withdrew from Agedadia. The DAK captured Msus on January 25 and Benghazi four days later. The British had lost 1,400 men and 100 tanks.

At the start of February 1942 the 8th Army dug itself into positions in Gazala. The defences consisted of a series of wired-in positions with minefields that were called "Boxes" that extended 80.4km (50 miles) inland. The weakness in these positions was that they were not mutually supporting and so could be reduced one at a time. The box at Bir Hacheim to the south was held by a Free French force commanded by the charismatic General Marie–Pierre Koenig and included men of the Foreign Legion.

In an operation code named *Venezia*, the 8th Army was attacked on May 27–28 by combined German and Italian forces. On May 31 in the Battle of the Cauldron Rommel outmanoeuvred the 8th Army, Operation *Aberdeen* was then launched by Ritchie to destroy the DAK supply lines. Using the phenomenal tank-killing power of the 8.8cm Flak gun Rommel halted the 8th Army attacks.

On June 11 Bir Hacheim had been under constant attack for ten days and the Free French forces finally withdrew. Their defence did much to restore the standing of French forces with the British following the defeat of 1940.

With only 100 tanks left the 8th Army was finally forced to retreat from Cyrenaica. This time Rommel was able to take Tobruk, now held by the 2nd South African Division, on June 21. He attacked from the south-east, an approach that was unexpected, and took 35,000 prisoners and vast stocks of supplies.

Churchill later referred to this as "one of the heaviest blows I can recall during the war" and had to face a censure motion in the House of Commons. In Berlin there was delight. Rommel was promoted to Field Marshal and lionised by the Nazi propaganda machine.

Ritchie's intention was to make a "do or die" stand at Mersa Matruh but Auchinleck saw the priority to keep the 8th Army intact. He sacked Ritchie on June 25 and took command. Auchinleck planned to stop Rommel at El Alamein but was also prepared to fight on in Palestine. On June 26 Field Marshal Albert Kesselring *OB Sud* (C-in-C South), Count Ugo Cavallero, the Italian Chief of Staff in Rome, and Marshal Ettore Bastico arrived at Rommel's HQ and gave him grudging permission to push on for Egypt.

ABOVE LEFT: General Claude Auchinleck (left) confers with General Neil Ritchie. Though Ritchie was relieved of the command of the 8th Army he commanded the XII Corps of the British 2nd Army in Europe with distinction.

ABOVE: Rommel in his SdKfz 250/3 *"Griffon"*, one of the vehicles in which he exercised front line command in North Africa. Radio signals from this half track would have been deciphered by the ULTRA teams.

LEFT: Cramped in a trench, *Afrika Korps* soldiers wait for the order to attack at Tobruk in 1942.

The Italians saw the ruthless approach to war causing mounting casualties among their forces and Rommel as a commander over which they had no control. Though he was a brilliant and aggressive leader, his drive to lead from the front meant that he was often out of contact with his HQ and staff.

On June 27 the DAK outflanked the Mersa Matruh position and a day later captured Fuqa. When Mersa Matruh fell on June 29 the Axis forces again captured huge stocks of supplies. Optimism among Axis leaders was high and Mussolini arrived in Libya to prepare for his triumphant entry into Cairo. In the desert there was confusion as 8th Army vehicles and Axis mingled in the move eastwards. This confusion was further compounded by the use by the *Afrika Korps* of captured trucks, tanks and artillery. When Rommel's forces arrived at the Alamein area on June 30 they caused panic in Cairo and moves to evacuate the city and move HQs and staff to Palestine. June 30 was known as "Ash Wednesday" as staffs began to burn classified papers.

Sandstorms, heavy artillery fire and attacks by the Desert Air Force slowed down Rommel's attacks on July 1. He mounted further attacks against El Alamein and Ruweisat Ridge but, exploiting ULTRA intelligence, Auchinleck attempted a counter stroke to the south.

In six weeks of confused fighting the 8th Army fought the Axis forces to a standstill and by July 3 the *Afrika Korps* had only 26 tanks fit for action. Churchill, aware that commanders in North Africa had access to ULTRA intelligence, was impatient at the apparent lack of progress and so on August 13 he replaced Auchinleck with General Harold Alexander as Commander in Chief Middle East with General Bernard Montgomery in command of the 8th Army.

LEFT: New Zealand and British troops wait in a PoW cage in Libya. This cage had been set up by the 8th Army and then captured by the *Afrika Korps*.

RIGHT: A 17cm K 18 in action. A Krupps-designed gun, it could fire a 68kg (150lb) shell to a maximum range of 28,000 metres (30,520yd) and had a dual recoil mechanism.

BELOW: Dust is kicked up by an 8.8cm gun as it fires against 8th Army tanks. The barrel of the gun has white "kill rings" to indicate how many tanks it has destroyed.

ABOVE: *Afrika Korps* logistics personnel fill metal water containers that are distinguished by the white cross on the black background.

Rommel's final throw was the battle of Alam Halfa that began on the night of August 30. He now had 200 German and 240 vulnerable Italian tanks but with low fuel stocks he was relying on capturing fuel from the 8th Army. The 8th Army now had 700 tanks, many of which were modern American Grants or Shermans. Rommel planned a feint to the north and then a hook round the flank to the south. With the benefit of ULTRA Montgomery anticipated this and the Axis forces were halted in two attacks on August 31 and September 1, and by September 2 the DAK were back to their start line.

The ability of the senior British comman-

ABOVE: A German 5cm Pak 38 anti-tank gun behind a sandbag sangar.

BELOW: An Axis patrol boat tied up at Tobruk harbour. Submarines and patrol boats operated extensively in the Mediterranean against shipping.

25-PDR MARK 2

The BritishTwenty Five Pounder gun/howitzer or Ordnance Q.F. 25-pdr Mark 2 on Carriage 25-pdr Mark 1 had a muzzle velocity of 532m/s (1,745 feet a second), a maximum range of 12,253m (13,400yds) and fired a 11.34kg (25lb) shell. Developed in the 1930s it first saw action in Norway in 1940. In North Africa, firing 9.07kg (20lb) steel shot, gunners fought almost point blank actions with Afrika Korps tanks. By 1945 the Royal Ordnance Factories had produced 12,000 25-Pounders and the gun would serve through the Korean war up to the conflict in Oman. The definitive gun is the 25-pounder Mark 3 which weighed 1801kg (3,968 lb) and had a distinctive Solothurn muzzle brake. All the guns were fitted with an innovative feature, a detachable circular platform on which the wheels rested, which allowed the crew of six to traverse the gun quickly through 360°.

ders to second guess the *Afrika Korps* and also to intercept vital convoys running between Italy and North Africa led Rommel to believe that there were traitors among the Italian staff who were in contact with the British. In reality, in North Africa, where the huge distances made radio vital for communications, it also laid the Germans open to interception and decryption. Just prior to Alam Halfa the Axis had lost four out of six supply ships that had sailed from Italy to North Africa. Though their movements had been tracked through ULTRA, the British always ensured that there was a cover story

RIGHT: A captured South African soldier looks glumly out of the cover of *Die Wehrmacht*.

BELOW: Rommel, with Lt Colonel Fritz Bayerlein, his chief of staff, in the background, receives a front line briefing.

ABOVE: A PzKpfw III protected by sandbags and extra track links moves along a desert track. The crew are seated on top to stay cool in the African sun.

to explain the interception. It was normally air reconnaissance – the aircraft would be seen by the German and Italian crews who would assume that was why they were subsequently attacked. Montgomery was criticised for using ULTRA too obviously in his deployments at Alam Halfa and possibly compromising it.

Stymied at Alam Halfa, the *Afrika Korps* dug in to await the 8th Army counter attack.

By October 23, 1942, Rommel had 80,000 men and 540 tanks, of which 280 were Italian and only 38 the superior PzKpfw IV.

Montgomery and Alexander, having resisted pressure from Churchill for an earlier attack, had amassed 230,000 men and 1,200 tanks, including 500 Grants or Shermans. It was time for the final show down between the 8th Army and the *Afrika Korps*.

The *Afrika Korps* had developed a belt of defences between the Mediterranean coast and the Quattara Depression, an area of salt marsh to the south that was reported to be impassable to vehicles. Though there were

ABOVE: 8th Army lorried infantry in a typical vehicle laden with personal kit and sand channels for unditching in soft sand, cross the Egyptian-Libyan border.

RIGHT: *Afrika Korps* soldiers examine a knocked out Lee/Grant tank. With this American-built vehicle the 8th Army was at last fielding reliable tanks with good armament that allowed them to engage German tanks at longer ranges.

P-40B TOMAHAWK IIA

Known in the USA as the Warhawk, the P-40 was used by France, the USSR and the RAF. The fighter was a derivation of the P-36 Hawk and entered service in 1939. It was followed by the P-40B and this type equipped RAF squadrons operating in North Africa. The airframe was upgraded with improved powerplants and enhanced armament, with the RAF operating the P-40E as the Kittyhawk IA. The P-40 played a significant role in the war in the Pacific.

Type:	Fighter
Crew:	1
Power Plant:	One 1,040hp Allison V-1710-33
Performance:	Maximum speed at 4,572m (15,000ft) 566km/h (352mph)
Maximum range:	1,980km (1,230miles)
Weights:	Empty 2,536kg (5,590lb) Loaded 3,447kg (7,600lb)
Dimensions:	Wing span 11.38m (37ft 4in) Length 9.67m (31ft 8in) Height 3.22m (10ft 7in)
Armament:	Two .50in (12.7mm) MG in engine cowling; two .30in wing mounted MG

natural obstacles in the desert – wadis, ridges and escarpments – these presented less of a threat to mobility than the deep minefields that were laid by both sides.

German minefields were marked with boards showing a skull, crossed bones, the letter "M" or the warning *Achtung Minen* –

'Attention Mines'. Barbed wire might be wrapped around fence posts in a distinctive pattern to indicate the edge of the minefield. Live minefields were marked with upright lettering and dummy fields with slanting. Throughout the war the markings were changed to confuse Allied intelligence.

LILI MARLEEN (LILLI MARLENE)

The song was based on the poem written by Hans Leip in Hamburg in 1923. Set to music in 1936 by Norbert Schultze it was sung by the Swedish-born singer Lale Anderson. Initially the Nazi propaganda authorities decided that its theme would be poor for morale and it was not broadcast. It was discovered by a presenter in German-controlled Radio Belgrade and when it was broadcast to the *Afrika Korps* it became an immediate hit – with the British 8th Army as well as German forces. It tells the story of the love of a soldier for his girl who waits for him outside the barracks. Translated, it was sung by Anne Sheldon to British troops, while the 1944 film *Lilli Marlene* starred Marlene Dietrich.

(Vor der Kaserne, vor dem großen Tor)

Worte: Hans Leip   Musik: Norbert Schultze

Vor der Kaserne, vor dem großen Tor
stand eine Laterne, und steht sie noch davor,
so wolln wir uns da wiedersehn. Bei der Laterne wolln wir stehn
:,: wie einst, Lili Marleen. :,:

Unsre beiden Schatten sahn wie einer aus.
Daß wir so lieb uns hatten, das sah man gleich daraus.
Und alle Leute solln es sehn, wenn wir bei der Laterne stehn
:,: wie einst, Lili Marleen. :,:

Schon rief der Posten, sie bliesen Zapfenstreich,
es kann drei Tage kosten, Kamerad, ich komm sogleich.
Da sagten wir auf Wiedersehn. Wie gerne wollt ich mit dir gehn,
:,: mit dir, Lili Marleen. :,:

Deine Schritte kennt sie, deinen schönen Gang,
alle Abend brennt sie, doch mich vergaß sie lang.
Und sollte mir ein Leid geschehn, wer wird bei der Laterne stehn
:,: mit dir, Lili Marleen? :,:

Aus dem stillen Raume, aus der Erde Grund
hebt mich wie im Traume dein verliebter Mund.
Wenn sich die späten Nebel drehn, werd' ich bei der Laterne stehn
:,: wie einst, Lili Marleen. :,:

Textabdruck mit Genehmigung des Apollo-Verlags Paul Lincke. Berlin SW 68.
Oranienstraße 64. Dieses Lied ist auch für Klavier – Gesang. Salon-Orchester.
Blasmusik. Akkordeon. Harmonika. Zither usw. erschienen.

MINE WARFARE

Landmines came in two types, anti-tank (AT) and anti-personnel (AP). The former were designed to explode when a tank or wheeled vehicle depressed the mechanism that operated the fuse. The latter were designed to kill or injure men and might disable a wheeled vehicle. AP mines fall into two classes – blast or fragmentation. In German use the former were designated *Schü-Minen* and the latter *Springen-Minen*, or *Schrapnellmine* or S mine. Mines were usually buried 50 to 100mm (2-4in) below the ground spaced at 2m (6ft 6in) interval

The S-Mine was a cylinder 5in (130mm) high, 4in (100mm) in diameter and weighed 4kg (9lb) It had a 395gm (14oz) TNT filling with a propelling charge of 226gm (8oz) of powdered TNT. It operated either by pressure of about 6.8kg (15lb) on the three prongs of an S.Mi.Z 34 igniter or by a pull on one of the two trip wires on the Z.Z.35 igniter that had been screwed into the top of the mine. This would release a spring-loaded striker that would fire a percussion cap. A delay of about 3.9 seconds would follow before the powdered TNT blasted an inner cylinder about 0.9m to 1.5m (3ft to 5ft) into the air. At this height it exploded and 360 ball bearings or chunks of mild steel rod were blasted in all directions causing death up to 20m (22yd) or injury up to 100.5m (110yd).

The *Schüminen* used the Z.Z.42 igniter with a No 8 Detonator screwed into a 1928 Pattern 200gm (7oz) TNT Slab Demolition Charge. The igniter and charge were fitted into a black compressed fibre container – the low metallic content would have made it harder to detect with

ABOVE: Tellermine 42.

ABOVE: S mine with Y adaptor.

ABOVE: Glass mine 43.

electronic mine detectors. Under pressure the Z.Z.42 igniter fired the detonator and when the main charge exploded it had a blast area of 10m (10.9yd).

The S-Minen were buried at 4m (13ft) intervals in lines while the *Schü-Minen* were buried at 1m (3.2 ft) intervals.

The *Tellermine,* literally "plate mine" because of its flat cylindrical appearance, was also known as the T-Mine and was the standard German anti-tank mine. During the war four versions were produced: the *Tellermine* 43 (Pilz) – "Mushroom", the *Tellermine* 1942, the *Tellermine* 35 and the *Tellermine* 29. They weighed 8.6kg (19lb), of which 5kg (11lb) was the TNT filling. T-Mines operated under a pressure of 108.9kg to 181kg (240lb to 400lb). The casing had threaded slots to take anti-handling pull switches, like the *Zugzünder* 35 that operated on a pull of between 4kg and 5.8kg (9lbs and 13lbs) and would detonate the mine if it was lifted by hand. The *Entlastungszünder* 44 pressure release device containing 226gm (8oz) of TNT-PETN could be positioned beneath the mine. It required a weight of 4.5kg (10lbs) to hold it safely in the armed position.

ABOVE: Tellermine 35.

The German minefields were in some areas almost 8km (5 miles) deep and besides a mixture of AT mines with AP mines to deter 8th Army engineers as well as kill or injure infantry, the *Afrika Korps* had even dug in 250kg (500lb) aerial bombs as massive anti - tank mines. In the dramatic language popular at the time, these complex minefields were dubbed "Devil's Gardens".

For Churchill a decisive British victory in North Africa was vital for political reasons before the United States became involved in fighting on land and became the "senior partner" in the war. Men and new machines would be pitted against the *Afrika Korps* at El Alamein. The high water mark of German operations in North Africa.

ABOVE: The beginning of the end for the *Afrika Korps* as captured soldiers are marched off to PoW camps. They had fought a hard but honourable campaign.

LEFT: Wrecked by a mine and possibly destroyed by its crew before they withdrew, is a gutted PzKpfw III. Rommel was now critically short of tanks.

INDEX